# The Computerization of
# Human Service Agencies

# THE COMPUTERIZATION OF HUMAN SERVICE AGENCIES

## A Critical Appraisal

John W. Murphy and John T. Pardeck

Auburn House

New York • Westport, Connecticut • London

Library of Congress Cataloging-in-Publication Data

Murphy, John W.
  The computerization of human service agencies : a critical
appraisal / John W. Murphy and John T. Pardeck.
    p.  cm.
  Includes bibliographical references and index.
  ISBN 0–86569–023–5 (alk. paper)
    1. Human services—Data processing.  I. Pardeck, John T.
II. Title.
HV29.2.M87  1991
361'.00285—dc20      90–22750

British Library Cataloguing in Publication Data is available.

Library of Congress Catalog Card Number: 90–22750
ISBN: 0–86569–023–5

First published in 1991

Auburn House, 88 Post Road West, Westport, CT 06881
An imprint of Greenwood Publishing Group, Inc.

Printed in the United States of America

The paper used in this book complies with the
Permanent Paper Standard issued by the National
Information Standards Organization (Z39.48–1984).

10  9  8  7  6  5  4  3  2  1

# Contents

# Preface

Seymour Papert is correct in his assessment of computer technology. In his words, computerization constitutes a set of "powerful ideas." Subsequent to the widespread acceptance of computers, new life has been interjected into social science. Due to the increased reliability and validity that are assumed to be derived from the use of computers, many social practitioners believe that their work will be enhanced. The claim is that if knowledge is power, computerizing social service programs should improve the status of clinicians, managers, and most other agency personnel.

Practitioners have found the lure of value-freedom difficult to ignore. But is any endeavor devoid of values? According to the argument advanced in this book, value-freedom is a chimera. That is, knowledge cannot be divorced from human action or interpertation. Yet most problematic, a naive belief in objectivity may serve to conceal assumptions that are made about reality. And, as many contemporary critics note, unexamined beliefs constitute nothing more than an ideology. Perhaps this is why many practitioners have been reluctant to criticize the use of computers in intervention, other than in technical terms. Nonetheless, most of the criticisms that have originated from this sector have not been very trenchant.

On the other hand, philosophers have been in the forefront of supplying insightful critiques of computer technology. And, clearly, social practitioners should be made aware of these issues. For despite a reluctance to acknowledge any relationship between philosophy and practice, these two spheres are not separate. The key contribution of this book, therefore, is to provide entree to a domain that is foreign to most practitioners.

Computers have a conceptual and philosophical basis that will adversely affect therapy and other forms of intervention, if these influences are not completely understood. This means topics must now be addressed—related to knowledge, values, and ethics—that were unheard of as recently as ten years ago. Having good intentions, an adequate action plan, and a rigorous evaluation scheme are no longer sufficient to insure that services are appropriately delivered. Conceptual acuity must also be achieved. Hopefully, this book will provide practitioners with an opportunity to sharpen their conceptual skills, with regard to adopting computer technology.

Special thanks go to Mrs. Emy Glass for typing the manuscript for our book. The authors also appreciate the typing assistance of Ms. Liew Pei King and Ms. Janette Haguewood.

# The Computerization of
# Human Service Agencies

# 1

# Introduction: Is Computerization a Philosophy or a Technique?

Some commentators argue that this is the Computer Age.[1] Accordingly, the most important commodity available is information. Practically every day a new device is created to process data. As a result, knowledge is gathered, manipulated, and disseminated with ever increasing efficiency. In this regard, Daniel Bell writes that the "codification of knowledge" is the new guiding principle of society.[2] Technical consultants who aid in this process are paid handsomely—business people, farmers, and many others regularly pay exorbitant sums of money for the most up-to-date information. Rapid access to information and a quick turn around time for data, moreover, are thought to lead to improved productivity. In sum, the efficient generation and transfer of information are treated as integral to the success of any endeavor.

In fact, Jacques Ellul asserts that a condition of "technological slavery" has begun to spread throughout society. By this he means that the influence of computers has begun to pervade practically every aspect of social life to such an extent that their absence is almost unimaginable. Furthermore, the instrumental or utilitarian outlook that is ubiquitous nowadays is thought to be a natural outgrowth of computerization. Mechanistic analogies and formalistic schemes are now de rigueur for describing society. Actually, interpretation and a lack of procedural rigor are assumed to un-dermine progress. Through the use of computers the control of any activity is allegedly enhanced, thereby further discrediting the hu-man element as a valid source of inspiration and knowledge. Thus dehumanization continues unabated. In other words, attendant to computerization is the view that so-called subjectivity is anathema to reliable decision making, in addition to almost any other activity. With regard to cybernetics, Langdon Winner notes that "self-gov-erning human will is now thought to be a tired anachronism".[3]

Computers have become integral to the operation of most or-ganizations. In fact, these machines are proliferating at an unprec-edented rate in every sort of business, for the utilization of computers is thought to improve the output of all workers. Even in the area of social service delivery, which is typically labor-intensive, emphasis has been placed on the use of computers. Due to Reaganomics and the accompanying retrenchment that has been witnessed in the past few years, the computerization of services has been encouraged to save money.[4] Along with efficiency, the quality of work is thought to be upgraded as a result of computers. After all, these devices continue to perform under any conditions in a routine manner. Hence the flow of information is streamlined and, for the most part, uninterrupted.

Computer programs are now available that can complete prac-tically any task in a social service agency. For example, in-take interviews, diagnostic assessments, training, and even therapy ses-sions can be computerized.[5] Computer–mediated therapy is thus no longer a fantasy. Working in an agency nowadays is almost impossible without understanding a wide range of high-tech in-struments. This trend, however, has not gone uncriticized.

Critics charge that dire consequences will result from the com-puterization of social services. They contend jobs will be lost, the workplace will come to resemble a factory, and the therapeutic relationship will be destroyed.[6] In short, the delivery of services may be seriously impaired or dehumanized. The purpose of this book, nonetheless, is not to sound the alarm that the use of com-puters should be abandoned. The authors are not neo-Luddites. Yet, certainly, some precautions are warranted; therefore, construc-tive criticism is offered.

What the authors encourage is the development of "socially responsible" technology. The point is that computers can be placed within a context that will allow them to be used in a socially sensitive manner. This concept is different from that advanced by E. F. Schumacher, who argues that technologies of appropriate scale are needed to avert the destruction of society. Socially responsible technologies are only spuriously related to a decrease in their size. The context of utilization, instead, is more important. In other words, the humane use of technology has little to do with technical issues. Ultimately significant is the environment into which computer technology is introduced. Computers should not be eliminated from agencies, but rather these devices should be better understood (made less autonomous). Related to this change in context are both practical and theoretical considerations.

Until now most of the critiques that have been forthcoming have focused on technical issues. Stated differently, the arguments against the use of computers in human services have been atheoretical. Actually, a reader might ask, what could be less theoretical than a computer? But such a view of computers would be wrongheaded and unproductive. As much of the current research on artificial intelligence (AI) illustrates, computerization and theory are closely interrelated.[7] Indeed, progress in this area is thought to be hampered because of unresolved theoretical questions. Given this failure, social practitioners would be wise to pay attention to the theoretical underside of computer operation.

A theme that has become increasingly significant is the computer "microworld." Understanding computers to be based on a particular world-view has profound social implications. Simply stated, computers are not value-free, contrary to popular opinion. Instead computers make demands on information and may even begin to shape the process whereby information is generated. When persons learn to operate a computer, for example, they are introduced to much more than technical considerations. Often overlooked is that they are expected to accept a particular way of conceptualizing reality that constitutes the computer microworld.[8]

In a manner of speaking, a unique cognitive style underpins computer use. And if practitioners are not careful, this way of construing reality may begin to influence a wide range of agency functions. At this juncture theory and practice are united. The demands imposed by the computer microworld may begin to alter how practitioners conceive of data, therapy, and other key aspects of service delivery. Hence computers should not be viewed simply as tools that are involved passively in an agency. In this sense, according to Albert Borgmann, "technology ... is the unspoken and invisible framework of discussion of values."[9] And as proponents of AI are discovering, the theoretical presuppositions of computerization are far reaching and often disruptive.

At this time, an important distinction must be made between computers and computerization. Whereas computers are machines, computerization provides the theoretical justification for their operation. Computers, in this sense, are tools. However, the tenets that sustain computer use are much more powerful than the actual hardware and software. And combined with computerization, computers become far more than tools. When practitioners purchase a computer, they also give legitimacy, albeit implicitly, to the mode of cognition that is referred to in this book as computerization. Moreover, the power of computers is derived from the theoretical principles that are at the heart of computerization. For this reason, Joseph Weizenbaum argues that the thrust of computers is not technological.[10] In this regard, Norbert Wiener declares that computers are nothing but information. This statement may sound odd to most persons, because they have been led to believe that technological advancements have made possible the use of computers. Nonetheless, the strength of computers lies with their conceptual basis. And the main shortcoming of computers, as Martin Heidegger might say, is that the philosophy that underpins this technology does not encourage thinking.

A point of clarification is necessary at this time. At issue is not whether a computer can be built to mimic the operations of the human mind. Instead, what Heidegger is saying is that the philosophical basis of computerization is believed to be beyond scrutiny. Technological rationality is treated as if it is universal and, moreover, the paragon of reason. Therefore, criticism of the theoretical presuppositions of technology is not deemed to be necessary. Correspondingly, computer technology gains a sense of autonomy; this technology appears to be justified by principles that are unquestioningly legitimate.

Offered in this book will be a critique of various computer applications. For each facet of service delivery that is addressed, both conceptual and practical shortcomings will be explored. Additionally, the link between theory and practice will be stressed. As should be noted, the remedies to the problems spawned by the implementation of computers are not simply technological. Logistical refinements may enhance the utility of computers, but the humanization of these devices is a theoretical concern. This point should never be ignored, for otherwise practitioners may become trapped within a never ending cycle of technology, which is referred to by Ellul as the "self-augmentation of technique." In other words, computer technology may become self-perpetuating, with no end to this process in sight.[11] Why should technological refinements be expected to cure the problems spawned by technology? In order to create a socially responsible technology, instead, the social significance of technical reason must be appreciated.

As might be expected from the foregoing discussion, chapter 2 will deal with the computer microworld.[12] In other words, the philosophy that underpins the operation of computers will be examined in detail. The epistemology that has come to fruition during the so-called Computer Age will be the focus of attention. This point of departure is deemed very important, considering that most practitioners approach computers as if they are simply machines.

It should be noted that the philosophy of computerization is not exactly new, although this way of thinking represents a quantum leap in the process described by Max Weber as the increasing "rationalization" of the world.[13] Without computerization, the operation of computers would be impossible. Accordingly, this chapter might be subtitled, "A walk through the computer microworld." For example, questions pertaining to the theory of knowledge, view of facts, conception of the mind, and social imagery that are a part of this outlook will be raised at this juncture. The use of "expert systems"—programs that outline the protocol for making a diagnosis—will be examined, in order to illustrate the impact of the computer microworld.[14] Emphasized will be how computerization can become a stifling ideology, as a result of "detach[ing] society's self-understanding from the frame of reference of communicative understanding and from the concepts of symbolic interaction."[15]

One of the key functions of computer technology is the organization of agencies. Most social service programs are not well regulated. Information can seldom be found when it is needed. Often a funding source will request a description of clients, details about the number and type of services provided, or data pertaining to the outcome status of clients, which managers are expected to provide in a short period of time. Paging through individual files is clearly not a reasonable solution to this problem. Furthermore, treatment plans are supposed to be revised periodically and the eligibility of clients for services must be checked almost hourly.

Chapter 3 will discuss the computer strategies that are supposed to enable practitioners and managers to "master the workflow of operations,"[16] for urgently needed is the ability to manage correspondence, track clients, update files, and evaluate treatment. The "routenization" of agencies, to use a concept popularized by Weber, will be the focus of attention. This term means that agencies are rendered predictable. This service can be supplied by computers because they are fast, do not haphazardly omit information, have long memories, and usually do what they are told. Hence various programs are now on the market that facilitate the efficient management of an office, but may ultimately result in increased bureaucratization.

In the following chapter, the organizational control of information will be analyzed further. Most often this is accomplished through the use of a management information system (MIS). In point of fact, in many agencies a MIS is viewed to be the solution to their data collection, storage, and utilization problems. When the flow of paper in an organization becomes unmanageable, managers and staff persons turn regularly to computers for help. Most workers believe that their access to information will improve, once manual information systems are updated through the implementation of computers. This optimism, however, is not necessarily warranted.

Most important for practitioners to remember is that a MIS represents a communication process. Before installing a MIS, therefore, the following question should be asked: Do functional communication channels exist in an agency? If not, effective communication networks must be (re)created by a MIS. Thus, for example, merely grafting computers on to a bankrupt communication network will not improve the flow of knowledge throughout an organization. Because a MIS embodies communication, issues that are essential to the successful exchange of information must be addressed, along with technical problems. The identity of data, the possible disruption of natural communication channels, learning curves, and the eventual destiny of information must receive serious consideration. Of course, cost, capacity, accessibility, and other technical points must also be raised. Yet practitioners should remember that the transmission of information is not simply a technical undertaking. If a MIS is treated as an aid to communication, this technology should be used for the purpose of enhancing interpersonal competence. Accordingly, the principle of communicative competence, as modern writers contend, should guide MIS development, rather than simply "systems analysis" that stresses transmitting information along an extremely structured pathway in the most expedient manner possible.

In this instance, communicative competence refers to understanding the reality that is operative in a particular setting, especially in terms of how this viewpoint is sustained through human effort. As some modern organizational analysts contend, within each agency a different culture may be present. An astute manager, therefore, will be aware of these differences when planning and assembling a MIS. The suggestion is that the culture of an organization should not be violated by a MIS. Otherwise, even a technically refined MIS may be terribly disruptive. What this means is the demands made by a MIS should not be inconsistent with the mode of reality construction that is central to the operation of an agency. When this is the case, Jürgen Habermas notes that the "inner logic of technical development" begins to shape and distort interaction.[17]

As many clinicians are aware, the therapeutic setting is currently being inundated by computers. The focus of chapter 5 will be the logistical side of this trend. Many technological adjuncts to therapy are on the market. These developments relate to conducting interviews, administering and scoring clinical instruments, monitoring treatment plans, and writing and reviewing case notes. Moreover, a variety of simulation games exist that are thought to facilitate discourse between a client and therapist. These enhancements have not been exceedingly controversial, although the administrating and scoring of tests has been cited as problematic.[18] When placed in the context of an adjunct to therapy, these computer applications may be relatively innocuous. The wisdom of the therapist, in short, remains the centerpiece of therapy. For as the term adjunct suggests, computers merely supplement a much more fundamental process.

Yet the claim is now being made in some circles that computer-mediated therapy is possible and even desirable.[19] Subsequent to this demarche, the status of computers changes appreciably. No longer are these devices at the periphery of the therapeutic encounter, but now the process of conducting therapy is shrouded in technology. The idea that computers could be intimately involved in therapy accompanied the development of DOCTOR and ELIZA. Due to recent innovations in computer technology, however, these programs are often treated as games. Available are much more powerful programs that can be used to assist clients in identifying and solving their problems. But, as might be expected, computer-mediated therapy announces the arrival of problems never before imagined.

In chapter 6, the authors analyze computer-mediated therapy. Some critics charge that when therapy is underpinned by computers, unique social and political problems arise. If, as opponents to this use of computers argue, technology constitutes an ideology, computerized therapy can become the most sophisticated means of social control yet devised. For instance, therapists may come to believe they have at their disposal an absolutely valid "second opinion," while few clients are going to question the wisdom of a computer-based diagnosis. Thus the "social life-world" of patients may be destroyed in the name of science.[20] In other words, the judgments of therapists may be given a patina of objectivity, even though a variety of biases may be operating. Obscured, in short, may be the fact that therapy is a social process and is replete with biases. When this occurs, a lot of harm can be inflicted on clients.

Related to the point about ideology is that computers are associated with knowledge most citizens do not comprehend. To be more exact, most persons are intimidated by computers. Interjecting these machines, accordingly, into the therapeutic relationship may give enormous power to therapists. What was once a symmetrical encounter, may suddenly become asymmetrical. Additionally, technically mediated therapy tends to be impersonal, because of the emphasis that is placed on standardization and objectification. But suggested by a host of post-World War II philosophies is that such insensitivity cannot be justified, for therapy is a thoroughly human enterprise. This controversy over the nature of therapy will also receive attention in chapter 6.

In addition to therapy, an entire organizat.on may be transformed by computer technology. The nature of knowledge, norms, interaction, and social imagery may change dramatically subsequent to the onset of computerization. Following the acceptance of computer logic and the logistics of computerization, the thought processes of practitioners and management styles may be adversely affected. As is suggested, these changes occur on two levels: the interpersonal and the organizational. For example, the use of space may be altered, in addition to clients being classified.

Much of the controversy surrounding this dehumanization relates to the issue of "de-skilling."[21] Stated simply, are the skills of practitioners improved or eroded subsequent to the introduction of computers into organizations? If therapists begin to rely on expert systems, will their clinical skills atrophy? After all, clinical insight may come to be viewed as an impediment to rendering sound judgments; this sort of idiosyncratic knowledge may come into conflict with the rationality exhibited by computers. Why rely on the whims of therapists, when computers can identify and propose solutions to problems in a standardized manner? De-skilling and other possible forms of alienation that may result from the use of computers will be discussed in chapter 7.

What is meant by the term alienation? Although this concept has been a part of Western philosophy for quite some time, subsequent to the work of Karl Marx it has gained notoriety. Typically when someone is identified as alienated, this means that his or her work and interpersonal relationships are no longer enjoyable. In addition to believing they cannot exert any control over their workplace, employees feel their work is not rewarding. Many critics charge that computer technology contributes to this condition.[22] In this sense, Weizenbaum writes "a computing system that permits asking only certain kinds of questions, that accepts only certain kinds of 'data', that cannot in principle be understood by those who rely on it, such a computing system has effectively closed many doors that were open before it was installed."[23] The alienating effects of computerization will be studied as part of the process of ascertaining why the use of computers may truncate intervention efforts.

As might be suspected, the use of computers by social practitioners poses many novel ethical questions.[24] Robert Nisbet makes this point when he writes that instituted along with technology is an "autonomous set of values."[25] Of course, issues arise related to confidentiality, patient access to information, and the safety of computerized records. These, however, are merely logistical considerations. Much more significant are the ways in which the therapeutic relationship may be altered unfavorably by computers. For example, because the thrust of computer-mediated therapy is procedural refinement, the assumption is that symptom identification, diagnostic decision making, and the monitoring of clients will improve if service delivery is formalized. Nonetheless, this formalization may result in the violation of clients' rights.

Many of the new ethical concerns related to computerized therapy stem from the stress that is placed on "technical competence." In other words, the acquisition of increased technical skills is presumed to correlate with better therapy. Inter-rater reliability is thought to improve, for example, once computerized protocol are utilized. By adhering to standardized diagnostic guidelines, the chances of mistreatment are believed to be reduced. Yet as Weizenbaum declares, good therapy is not necessarily related to technical expertise![26] To confuse therapy with a technical exercise may culminate in increased insensitivity. Practitioners should remember that accuracy and precision are not necessarily synonymous. For a diagnosis that is precise may be socially inaccurate and, thus, irrelevant or possibly harmful. Moreover, the insensitivity associated with computerization may reverse the progress that has been made lately with regard to protecting the dignity of clients.

In chapter 8 the ethical concerns stemming from the use of computers will be surveyed. Perhaps most important, the ethical consequences attendant to the theoretical shifts announced by computerization will be given serious attention. Doubtless, when dealing with the topic of ethics the philosophy of computerization becomes of paramount importance.

The criteria for a socially responsible technology are suggested in chapter 9. As is suggested earlier in this introduction, a technology that can be readily integrated into social life is both technically and conceptually sound. The argument proposed in this book is that only a reflexive technology can be humanistic. Nonetheless, most often technical solutions are given primacy in terms of correcting the difficulties that may result from technology, for reflexivity is either not understood or dismissed. This traditional modus operandi, however, may generate more problems than remedies. In order for persons to gain control of technology, much more is needed than merely an increased mastery of the techniques involved. In short, the technological rationality or instrumental reason that sustains technology must be tempered. Saving technology relates to subjecting it to a critical analysis, in the manner suggested by Heidegger.[27] Building reflexivity into computerization constitutes the new challenge in using computers, and thus introducing the element of self-criticism into the operation of computer technology will prove to be very important in the future.

Practitioners should remember that computer design is more than simply a technical job; social and technical systems cannot be easily separated. As implied by the idea of computerized support systems, technological reasoning is not context-free. The purpose of computer technology is to interface with social conditions—autonomous technology makes no sense theoretically or practically. Therefore, practitioners should never lose sight of the social context of technological reason. They should not be thrust naively into the device paradigm, the key characteristics of which are extreme quantification, abstraction, commodification, efficiency, functional design, and manipulation.[28] But if computerization is treated as a social process, technical rationality, and thus computers, can be integrated into an agency without these dire consequences. By focusing on social contingencies, the limits of technical reason can be readily exposed and questioned. Computer use can become humane, because the reification of service delivery can be avoided.


## NOTES

1. Jean-Francois Lyotard, *The Postmodern Condition: A Report on Knowledge* (Minneapolis: University of Minnesota Press, 1984), pp. 1-4.
2. Daniel Bell, "Notes on the Post-Industrial Society." in *The Tech-*

*nological Threat*, ed. Jack D. Douglas (Englewood Cliffs, NJ: Prentice-Hall, 1971), p. 12.

3. Langdon Winner, *Autonomous Technology* (Cambridge: MIT Press, 1977), p. 16.

4. Howard Karger, "The De-skilling of Social Workers: An Examination of the Industrial Mode of Production and the Delivery of Social Services," *Journal of Sociology and Social Welfare*, 13 (1) (1986): pp. 115-129.

5. John T. Pardeck and John W. Murphy, "Microcomputer Technology in Clinical Social Work Practice," *ARETE* 11(1) (1986): pp. 35-43.

6. John T. Pardeck, Karen Collier Umfress, and John W. Murphy, "The Use and Perception of Computers by Professional Social Workers," *Family Therapy* 14(1) (1987): pp. 1-8.

7. Hubert L. Dreyfus, and Stuart E. Dreyfus, *Mind over Machine* (New York: The Free Press, 1986).

8. John W. Murphy, John T. Pardeck, Wesley L. Nolden, and Joseph J. Pilotta, "Conceptual Issues Related to the Use of Computers in Social Work Practice," *Journal of Independent Social Work* 1(4) (1987): pp. 63-73.

9. Albert Borgmann, *Technology and the Character of Contemporary Life* (Chicago: University of Chicago Press, 1984), p. 81.

10. Joseph Weizenbaum, *Computer Power and Human Reason* (San Francisco: W. H. Freeman, 1976), pp. 73-110.

11. William Leiss, *The Domination of Nature* (Boston: Beacon Press, 1974), pp. 113-124.

12. John W. Murphy and John T. Pardeck, "The Technological World-View and the Responsible Use of Computers in the Classroom," *Journal of Education* 167(2) (1985): pp. 98-108.

13. Max Weber, *Economy and Society*, vol. 2 (Berkeley: University of California Press, 1978), pp. 956-1005.

14. John W. Murphy and John T. Pardeck, "Nontechnical Correctives For High-Tech Systems in Social Service Agencies," *Clinical Supervisor* 6(2) (1988): pp. 63-73.

15. Jürgen Habermas, *Toward a Rational Society* (Boston: Beacon Press, 1970), p. 105.

16. Richard M. Kesner, *Information Systems* (Chicago: American Library Association, 1988), p. 2.

17. Habermas, *Toward a Rational Society*, p. 106.

18. Joseph D. Matarazzo, "Computerized Clinical Test Interpretations: Unvalidated Plus All Mean and No Sigma," *American Psychologist* 41(1) (1986): pp. 14-24.

19. Wesley L. Nolden, "Technology and Transference: Computers in

Psychotherapy," in *Technology and Human Productivity*, ed. John W. Murphy and John T. Pardeck (Westport, CT: Quorum, 1986), pp. 67-75.

20. Habermas, *Toward a Rational Society*, p 52.

21. Harry Braverman, *Labor and Monopoly Capital* (New York: Monthly Review Press, 1974), pp. 169-183.

22. Ibid., pp. 3-41.

23. Quoted in David Burnham, *The Rise of the Computer State* (New York: Random House, 1983), p. 151.

24. Lisa A. Callahan and Dennis R. Longmire, "The Role of Reason in the Social Control of Mental Illness," in *The Underside of High-tech*, ed. John W. Murphy, Algis Mickunas, and Joseph J. Pilotta (Westport, CT: Greenwood, 1986), pp. 53-65.

25. Robert Nisbet, "The Impact of Technology on Ethical Decision-Making," in *The Technological Threat*, pp. 39-54.

26. Weizenbaum, *Computer Power and Human Reason*, p. 270.

27. Terry Winograd and Fernando Flores, *Understanding Computers and Cognition* (Norwood, NJ: Ablex, 1986), pp. 163-179.

28. Borgmann, *Technology and the Character of Contemporary Life*, pp. 40-48.

# 2

# The Technological World-View, Western Philosophy, and Knowledge

## COMPUTER MICROWORLD

Margaret Boden notes correctly that computers do not simply "crunch numbers, but manipulate symbols."[1] An identical point is made by J. David Bolter when he suggests that subsequent to the work of Turing, Western culture was changed forever.[2] What these and other writers are claiming is that the desire to computerize information requires the adoption of new cultural imagery. To use a term popularized by Kuhn, a unique "paradigm" is given legitimacy, at least tacitly, in order for the computerization of knowledge to be successful.[3] Symbolism that is compatible with computer use, in other words, has been invented. Yet the entire realm of symbolism indigenous to computerization is mostly overlooked by practitioners.

In a manner of speaking, computers "read" information. Input is introduced, classified, manipulated, and transformed into output. This process resembles cognitive activity. Yet not all information can be perceived by a computer; knowledge must assume a particular form. In short, only particular input can be recorded by a computer. This requirement does not pertain directly to content but to form, although the former may be gradually affected. Consequently, the question that becomes paramount is: Are the epistemological restrictions imposed by computerization legitimate, particularly when they are applied to the delivery of social services?

One thing a computer cannot tolerate is ambiguity. Therefore, input must have exact parameters, for knowledge that is vague defies classification. But classification is at the heart of computerization! As described by Bolter, computerization is impossible unless data can be assigned an address space within the memory of a computer.[4] Knowledge can be registered only after the criteria for this kind of placement have been met. In this regard, the cognitive categories that are present in a program are analogous to the mailboxes found in the vestibules of apartment houses. Only information that can be pigeonholed neatly can be computerized. Otherwise, a piece of input may be categorized in a variety of ways, thereby causing confusion. Every assignment of information must be clear and concise, or data will be rejected. But this process appears to be quite rarefied, for as the Dreyfuses conclude, "brains don't seem to decompose either language or images in this way."[5]

To comply with this requirement, however, a novel mode of classification was invented. Every sort of knowledge would be referred to as bits. In point of fact, the information bit is understood to be hallmark of the Computer Age.[6] The hope is that if input could be reduced to bits without any appreciable loss of meaning, the success of computers would be guaranteed. But does knowledge arrive in neatly packaged units? Critics of computerization contend that this view of knowledge is erroneous. Moreover, the formalization of information required by computerization is believed by many computer experts to be impeding advances in the area of artificial intelligence (AI). What is the justification, nonetheless, for viewing knowledge to consist of discrete chunks of information?

The success of digitalization is thought to hold the key to development of modern computers. Translated into symbolic terms, knowledge is characterized as $A = A, B = B$, and A does not equal B.[7] Suggested by this conception of information is that knowledge consists of objects, which are loosely connected. Moreover, events are understood to be reducible to their elementary parts, without any loss of meaning using concepts related to physics. Terry Winograd describes this viewpoint by saying that these basic units are thought to be the atoms or particles on which real knowledge is built.[8] And because these units are self-contained, each one has an identity that cannot be mistaken for any other. With each unit neatly circumscribed, the classification of data can proceed smoothly. No doubt should exist pertaining to where a piece of information belongs; each datum has a location that should not be occupied by any other kind of input.

When digitalization is put into practice, this mode of conceptualization becomes binary logic. Accordingly, input is identified as either 0 or 1. Conceptualizing knowledge in this way allows data to be transmitted smoothly along circuits, so that electrical switches can be triggered. If a 1 is present a switch is opened, whereas a 0 does nothing. While a series of open and closed switches may mean nothing to an uninformed onlooker, a particular arrangement of switches has both technical and *social* significance in terms of programming a computer. In other words, various patterns of 0s and 1s may have very different meanings. As should be noted, through the use of these switches, cognitive operations are supposedly duplicated.

The question that remains is whether or not digitalization provides an adequate portrayal of social life. Can knowledge be defined as "quantities of information," as Lyotard states, without dire consequences?[9] Opponents of computerization say no. They argue that input should not be described as "context-independent, objective features of the real world."[10] Another critic made this point by stating that the separation of signs from symbols—an essential tactic to computerize language—is not done in everyday life.[11] Their point is that they believe knowledge does not exist *sui generis*, but is embedded within layers of interpretation. Knowledge, stated differently, is context-bound and is seriously misrepresented when it is construed to be free of values, or a "thing". Yet with respect to computerization, information is thoroughly materialized. Accordingly, social practitioners should ask, can the world be depicted adequately as a series of 0s and 1s? Is the richness of social life underestimated, as a consequence of this maneuver?

Nonetheless, subsequent to the acceptance of digitalization, dualism reigns supreme. The separation of knowledge from subjectivity is not only deemed possible, but is applauded. Without equivocation, objectified facts or bits are considered to represent valid knowledge. Furthermore, computer space is thought to provide a framework wherein data can be classified without much trouble, because an abstract environment is available for storing information. Through computerization the impression is created that the human element is unimportant for classifying events. As long as data are explicitly defined and handled in a formalistic manner, the generation of undistorted information is assumed to be possible. Readers should take special note that a major consequence of digitalization is the neutralization of the data generation process. Meaning, as described by Claude Shannon and Warren Weaver, is systematically transformed into information with no regret.[12] As might be suspected, the latter has nothing to do with the semantic aspects of communication. The illusion is perpetrated, in other words, that knowledge unsullied by interpretation can be produced. In this regard, Ashley Montagu has reinterpreted the GIGO principle to mean "Garbage In, Gospel Out."[13]

The rapid either-or categorization of data is made possible as a consequence of accepting the computer microworld. Suggested by the concept microworld is that using computers presupposes the validity of a specific way of constructing reality. Three interrelated tenets are vital to maintaining this world-view.[14] As a result, a particular philosophy paves the way for technical advancements; a unique mode of conceptualization makes the computerization of phenomena appear to make sense. First, events should be conceived as things or objects, with little or no loss of meaning. Second, these factors should be quantified, because mathematics is a precise and neutral language. In this way, input will in all likelihood never be misunderstood. And third, the laws of formal logic should be employed at all times when manipulating data. Taken together, these rules almost guarantee the uninterrupted processing of information, for interpretation and other situational factors are allegedly excluded from the operation of a computer.

Implied by the computer microworld are a few additional ideas that will eventually prove to be very important.[15] Of particular note, logistical rigor is touted to lead naturally to the collection of high quality data. Accordingly, the standardization brought about by methodological refinements is thought to culminate in the generation of valid knowledge. If a behavior can be assumed to have objective features and follow precise rules, the belief is that this activity can be successfully computerized.[16] Consequently, accuracy and precision are presumed to be synonymous.

Another crucial point is that a distinction is made between objective and subjective data. In other words, hard and soft knowledge are believed to be very different. Simply stated, anything that defies quantification and transformation into brute matter is eschewed. Knowledge that is associated with interpretation, for example, is given a low priority. In the world of digitalized data, facts are differentiated from values without question. Input is thus "overcoded;" data are prevented from fluctuating.[17]

Last but not least, reason is oversimplified and presumed to be universal. Rationality is equated with internal consistency and the ability to distinguish clearly the objective features of nature. As the Dreyfuses report, reason has come to be known as *ratio*, rather than *logos*, and, thus, humans are thought to be uniquely adept at "counting and measuring."[18] Hence skill at perfecting a classificatory scheme is considered to be indicative of rational behavior. Furthermore, because the focus of attention is technical refinement, issues pertaining to the contextual character of reason are seldom raised. Identifying, classifying, and manipulating data are accepted as the key traits of a rational person. That reason may encompass appreciably more than technical consideration is not given much credence.

Especially relevant at this juncture is that the activity whereby data are identified and utilized is systematically deanimated.[19] Social factors are, at best, thought to be indirectly associated to the production of usable knowledge. Although this sentiment is epitomized by computerization, this viewpoint is not entirely new. Throughout the history of Western philosophy, knowledge untrammeled by opinion has been sought. Subsequent to the advent of computerization, however, the chances of discovering this exalted information are believed to improve. But in order to appreciate the place of digitalized knowledge in Western thought, the various ways in which true knowledge has been conceived must be recalled. The following section of this chapter is devoted to illustrating why computerization is a logical outgrowth of Western philosophy.

## ABSTRACT KNOWLEDGE AND WESTERN THOUGHT

Since the time of the early Greeks, an indubitable ground has been pursued to sustain knowledge and order. For this reason, Niklas Luhmann contends that Westerners have had a penchant for conceptualizing knowledge in a "centered" manner.[20] For unless the basis of knowledge is protected from interpretation, society would certainly dissolve into chaos. Knowledge and a reliable order are thus not subjective. Something as vital as truth could not be derived from interpretation, or any source equally as fragile, according to traditional Western thinkers.

For example, Plato argued for the existence of eternal ideas (or forms), which he believed underpinned the illusions encountered in everyday life. This absolute foundation is manifested in the work of Plato's student Aristotle in numerous ways. In general, he formulated a theory in which causality is unaffected by situational factors. Yet, much more relevant to computerization, Aristotle suggested that events could be classified neatly if logic were formalized. Indeed, his Law of the Excluded Middle represents an early attempt to establish a binary system of classification. As he suggests, if A does not equal B, then assigning events to categories would be relatively easy. For Aristotle every event has a self-contained identity $(A = A)$.[21] Following this maneuver, logical space is removed from the uncertainty that plagues interpretation.

Although Plato and Aristotle pursued unadulterated knowledge, their theories were imbued with mysticism and a plethora of speculative elements. During the medieval period these metaphysical themes continued, although at times debate occurred over the type of logic that was most appropriate. Ubiquitous to this period of philosophy, nonetheless, was an overriding concern to supply knowledge and order with a firm foundation. Yet placing Gods and revelation at the center of this activity were not very productive. Gods and demons, in short, inspire passion, as opposed to reason.

With the demise of medieval speculation circa 1600, modern rationalism was born.[22] Accordingly, a host of concepts were developed that would eventually foster computerization. With the appearance of Descartes, dualism was seen as unquestionably legitimate. Mind and world could be separated with no adverse consequences. Actually, overcoming the limitations imposed by consciousness was thought to be a prerequisite for the discovery of apodictic knowledge. Beyond the influence of interpretation was thought to exist a universe based on fact.

Once dualism became fashionable, the way was cleared for unlimited system building. Newton, for instance, proposed that the universe was organized in terms of absolute space, which came to be known as the *sensorium Dei*.[23] Following this precedent, the move to computer space was not very difficult. What Newton did was to say that a context existed in which the interrelationship between events could be monitored without a concern for situational contingencies. Indeed, he viewed the world to operate with clock-work precision. Further, the reason that guided the universe was infinite and not subject to interpretation. In this sense, rational systems and persons function with respect to uniform laws; idiosyncrasies are anathema to Newton's framework.[24]

As is suggested, diminishing the importance of the human element encouraged the proliferation of mechanistic renditions of how the universe, including humans, operates. For example, sixteenth and seventeenth century astronomers popularized the use of mathematics and tried to pinpoint the exact position and movement of planets. But at this time the development of the mechanical clock contributed most to the future growth of computerization. These devices were also known as calculating clocks. Central to these instruments is that the passage of time can be simulated through the turning of gears. Time, therefore, is made into a quantifiable or readily measurable unit. The point is that if something as elusive as time could be measured nothing is immune to quantification, even abstractions can be fit into such cognitive categories. Keeping this idea in mind, Pascal and Leibniz created what are believed to be the first mechanistic calculators.[25] In these examples, numbers were also thought to be represented sufficiently by turning gears. Hence number also became a technical construct.

Besides demonstrating that numbers could be identified and accumulated mechanistically, Leibniz made another contribution to computerization. As is well known, he envisioned the universe to be comprised of self-contained elements, known as monads. Thus knowledge is presumed to consist of bits and pieces of information. He believed a phenomenon is either a monad or it is nothing. Knowledge either has a positive presence or it constitutes a void. In modern terminology, knowledge is either a 1 or 0.[26] Thus everything has a simple identity that can be determined numerically. Leibniz rendered concrete—that knowledge is absolute and circumscribable—what remained unresolved in earlier philosophies. Furthermore, he maintained that a universal language could be derived from the knowledge revealed in monads. This belief in the existence of a uniform language would eventually fuel interest in developing computer language.

Another development occurred around the turn of the seventeenth century that further enhanced the prospects for computerization. Simply put, empiricism was beginning to become sophisticated.[27] Instead of abstract monads, knowledge was thought to be predicated on sense data. Knowledge, in other words, is envisioned to consist of nothing more than objective qualities. Due to their objective stature, these data are easily identifiable and create distinct impressions on the mind. Moreover, the mind tabulates the imprints that are left behind; the mind functions as a calculator. As Hobbes states, mental activity is expressed mostly through reckoning—the mechanistic "addition of parcels" and "substraction of one sum from another."[28] This depiction of knowledge and the mind convinced many later writers that an intelligent machine could be built. For if the mind operated like a machine, a cognitive computer could surely be constructed.

While Leibniz outlined the rudiments of a universal logic, the complete formalization of thinking did not occur until the work of the logical positivists appeared. Building on the systems invented by Boole and Frege, the attempt was made by positivists to transform logic into an ensemble of neutral signs.[29] Judgments, stated differently, were articulated in the form of technical operations. Through this maneuver the impression was created that information could be identified and utilized without the influence of passion. Hence logic machines were certainly within the realm of possibility. As Shannon and Weaver proceeded to illustrate, discrete bits of information could be joined and subsequently separated in a dispassionate manner. As a result even symbols could be neutralized. Machines that do not merely classify, but channel and respond on the basis of different types of input seemed feasible.

Additionally, the formalization of mathematics guaranteed that computerization would have a future. For example, David Hilbert claimed that mathematics is a formal system, consisting of axioms, inference rules, and theorems. But the formalism pursued by Hilbert could never be achieved, according to Gödel, for every theorem is finite. As is noted by Gödel, once a theorem is closed, the complete formalization of an axiom is precluded by definition. Therefore, the total formalization of thought would have to proceed differently.

Bertrand Russell and Alfred North Whitehead adopted another tack to addressing this issue. Instead of trying to show that mathematics is a comprehensive system, they set out to prove, at what might be called the microlevel, that $1 = 1$. If this statement is true, the classification of data is unproblematic. In a manner consistent with the Law of Excluded Middle, demonstrating mathematically that events have a single and irrefutable identity contributed significantly to the computerization of knowledge. Although their work has been criticized, Russell and Whitehead persuaded many persons that reality could be successfully formalized. Once facts become isomorphic with their empirical traits, numbers can adequately capture the meaning of events. In short, 1 is equal to 1 and nothing else. Accordingly, every event has a selfsame identity.

The aim of this historical excursus is not to be exhaustive, but to illustrate that the attempt has been made continually to eliminate the human element from the discovery of knowledge. And computerization represents the denouement of this tendency. In other words, Western philosophy has been characterized as a metaphysical tradition that culminates in technology. From the foregoing exposition the rationale for this conclusion should be clear. Computer space, for example, embodies the indivisible and absolute *archē*, or anchor for reality, that has been traditionally sought. The source of the One, the Good, and the True has been located at last.

A few questions should be asked at this juncture. Can dualism be theoretically justified? Many contemporary writers insists that knowledge cannot be severed categorically from the decisions persons make about their lives.[30] They claim that knowledge is misconstrued unless the existential or interpretive trust of information is recognized. Additionally, does the mind merely mimic reality and simply classify events? Again the answers is no according to the critics of this attempt to mechanize cognition. This debate over the stature of facts and mental activity is nowhere more apparent than in the work currently underway on expert systems. At the heart of this controversy is whether or not the human mind and decision making can be computerized effectively.

## COMPUTERIZATION, EXPERT SYSTEM, AND KNOWLEDGE

The purpose of an expert system is to replicate the decision making abilities of experts, minus the human error associated with interpretation. Programs have been available for some time that are capable of playing games, such as checkers. This technology is now being applied to a variety of medical and clinical tasks. Programs such as Internist, Dendral, Mycin, and Emycin are now widely used. Moreover, diagnostic schemes such as the DSM-III have been designed to be readily programmable. As a result, interviews can be performed via the computer, with judgements rendered that are believed extremely reliable. In sum, expert systems are thought to make possible "computer-aided decisions based on more wisdom than any one person can contain."[31]

Since the 1950s, the relevance of clinical insight for making a diagnosis has been considered suspect. In point of fact, one writer has gone so far as to claim that statistical predictions are more accurate than those made by trained clinicians.[32] The problem of basing clinical judgments on insight and experience relates to the issue of low inter-rater reliability. In short, identical symptoms are often interpreted differently by different clinicians. Diagnoses, therefore, appear to be made capriciously, thereby jeopardizing the scientific status of practitioners. After all, who wants the identity of their problem to depend on the whims of a therapist? As might be suspected, standardizing the diagnostic process is thought to be a way of resolving this issue. This solution appears to be logical, considering the history of Western thought. Expert systems, accordingly, are assumed to facilitate making informed judgements.

Obviously many routine decisions can be made more accurately by a machine than by humans. Highly questionable, however, is whether diagnoses should be approached in this manner. Nonetheless, through what Edward Feigenbaum calls "knowledge engineering," software packages have been developed that routenize a host of decision making processes.[33] As a result of interviewing experts, the protocol they use to judge information is installed as the knowledge base of a program. In terms of the DSM-III, for example, a team of psychologists was impaneled for the purpose of identifying various clinical syndrome and the steps that should be followed in diagnosing each one. Once this information was gathered, an attempt was made to design a framework that details how an expert clinician is expected to behave when faced with a particular pattern of symptoms.

All this sounds so simple. As a result of formulating a series of if/then statements—which constitutes an inferential engine—computers appear to have the ability to react intelligently to events. For instance, if A is presented, then B will be the computer's response. Following the implementation of these structural primitives, the stage is set for decisions to be rendered mechanistically.[34] In other words, the if/then statements serve to structure the search strategy of any informed clinician. Roger Schank and Robert Abelson refer to these standardized scenarios as "scripts."[35] Their terminology is very instructive: diagnoses are made by adhering to rigidly defined cognitive routines.

As should be noted, a stereotypical reply is elicited by input; prototypical factors delimit the boundaries of rational search behavior. But Terry Winograd argues, this modus operandi results in decision making that is quite "brittle."[36] MYCIN, a program designed to detect infectious diseases, particularly bacterial infections in the blood, unfolds in the following manner:

*If*: (1) The site of the culture is blood, and

(2) The gram stain of the organism is gramming, and

(3) The morphology of the organism is rod, and

(4) The patient is a compromised host

*Then*:  There is suggestive evidence (.6) that the identity of the organism is pseudomonas-aeruginosa.

This type of questioning continues until a full range of physical factors is addressed. As the answers that are given begin to distinguish one disease from another, an etiology is established. Finally, a probability statement is generated pertaining to the likelihood that a particular set of symptoms fits into a syndrome.

Once certain principles are accepted as valid, making a diagnosis is streamlined and relatively easy using these programs. Stated simply, axioms are applied to individual cases, in order to classify the traits that are revealed in each instance. Clearly this procedure will improve inter-rater reliability, for judgments are produced by following step-by-step instructions. As a result of adhering to precise directions, every competent clinician should reach a similar conclusion about a client's malady. Judgments are not haphazard, because a logic tree that specifies rational alternatives guides the evaluation of input. Making a diagnosis thus becomes a technical exercise.

Hubert and Stuart Dreyfus write that expert systems may produce reliable decisions, yet the issue of validity or legitimacy is certainly in doubt.[37] They argue persuasively that the operation of the mind has been misconstrued by advocates of expert systems. Basic to the operation of these systems are several assumptions that are dubious. Hubert Dreyfus refers to these as the biological, psychological, epistemological, and ontological assumptions.[38] As should be noted, the influence of the computer microworld is revealed through these tacitly made claims.

Central to the biological assumption is that the mind can be characterized as a network of off/on switches. Human understanding, accordingly, is the product of electrical impulses that are correlated with input. Presented with a bit of information, or a stimulus, the mind reacts in an all or none fashion that can be expected from a normal individual. The mind, in other words, registers 0s and 1s, channels these inputs appropriately, and emits a correct response.

That knowledge can be envisioned as bits of information, organized according to formal rules, is the thrust of the psychological assumption. Suggested by this viewpoint is that humans are simply rational, as argued by Herbert Simon.[39] Consistent with what empiricists believe, reason consists of a process whereby clearly described entities are enumerated. The mind, in this sense, functions like a grand calculator. Hence, data with exact parameters are simply classified and tallied. Processing information is thus presumed to be the primary cognitive activity.

Essential to the epistemological assumption is that knowledge can be formalized, without any appreciable distortion. The aim of this formalization is to create rules of reasoning that are divorced from extenuating circumstances. Therefore, laws of reason or logic are proposed that allegedly constitute the paragon of rationality. As a result of following these rules, logical conclusions are reached with regularity. Rationality is no longer elusive, but is nothing more that a style of thinking that any technically competent person can achieve. Becoming rational is as simple as reading a logic tree.

According to the ontological assumption, knowledge is defined as "discrete, explicit, and determinate data."[40] Most important is that knowledge is associated with the obtrusive features of events. As might be expected, data that appear to be objective are highly valued. The symbolic or interpretive side of knowledge acquisition is downplayed, because reliable information is unrelated to judgments. Stability is thought to be indicative of objectivity, and thus the uncertainty associated with interpretation is criticized. The focus of any undertaking, therefore, should be the rigorous operationalization of concepts and procedures.

Sustaining the drive to develop expert systems is the idea that the mind and computers are somehow alike. Yet is the mind nothing more than an analytical engine? Those who question the efficacy of this application of computerization say no. They believe that the mind should not be reduced to an apparatus that efficiently follows instructions. Mental activity, these critics charge, is not portrayed adequately by this model. Instead of simply reacting to events, the mind interacts with the world.

There is little doubt about the precision of the calculations generated by computerized clinical systems, yet critics maintain that the knowledge base of this technology is too abstract. More to the point, the knowledge invoked by expert systems to substantiate decisions is accumulated *without learning*.[41] As should be recognized, the ability to deduce a course of action from higher-order principles is considered to be the key characteristic of reason. But as described by Winograd and Flores, the deliberately restricted nature of formal logic creates blindness, in that relevance is determined on the basis of preselected factors that delimit even feedback.[42] In this sense, unexpected findings that are essential to expanding and creating a socially sensitive knowledge base are excluded from a person's repertoire or experiences. Clearly, following the steps prescribed by an algorithm is not the same as cognition! For cognition is not this passive during the process whereby knowledge is accumulated.

Contrary to this sterile version of cognition, Hubert and Stuart Dreyfus contend that reason is enacted through the ways in which persons interact with their environment. Reason does not exist in a vacuum, despite what is suggested by the use of expert systems. Persons, in short, define or interpret reality long before the ability to follow instructions is deemed to be important. Furthermore, these commentators declare that expert systems do not behave in a manner similar to experts.[43] They note that a novice classifies events on the basis of their empirical traits, and acts as if facts are context-free. Beginners focus on technical issues, regardless of the setting in which a task is undertaken. An expert, on the other hand, does not make a job conform to a single format. Experts have the ability to recognize the unique features of each situation, are able to compare cases, and can respond in a situationally sensitive fashion, while generating rules about how to handle a typical event. Learning when and when not to apply rules is part of becoming an expert, in addition to understanding when rules should be expanded in order to deal with new and unique problems. Put into concise terms, the search behavior of experts is not limited by artificially established guidelines.

In sum, experts are not reductionistic, as are expert systems. Rather than adopting a value-free stance, experts appreciate that knowledge is embroiled in the activities whereby reality is socially constructed. Experts are holistic, while novices are not. And because the vital element of interpretation is eliminated from expert systems, the complexity of knowledge acquisition is underestimated by these devices. Misconstrued is the myriad of ways in which persons interact with or socially construct their environment, and thus the limits that are placed on generalizing about rationality are given little attention. Expert systems proceed as if making judgments is not a social process.

## KEY CONCERNS RELATED TO COMPUTERIZING SOCIAL SERVICES

Clearly, significant social imagery accompanies the utilization of computers. Computers, in this sense, supply their own data selection guidelines. The attempt has been made in this chapter to illustrate why only specific types of knowledge can be successfully computerized. Why placing so much emphasis on formalization unduly truncates the number of possible sources of knowledge has also been discussed. And due to this narrow focus, knowledge can be easily reified through computerization, claim the critics of this technology.

What does reification mean in this discussion? In answer to this query, the identification and application of knowledge are given a technical cast. Following instructions faithfully is thought to lead naturally to the generation of reliable data and sound decisions. Furthermore, criticism is systematically moved to the periphery of these activities, because classificatory schemes are unsettled by questions. Essentially anything that cannot be translated into a series of technological operations has no utility in the computer microworld. In fact, writes Bolter, "men and women of the electronic age ... are indeed remaking themselves in the image of their technology."[44] Hence the idea that knowledge and social relations cannot be conceived in mechanistic terms is not taken seriously. Such myopia, however, may result in undermining social intervention.

For example, a person is portrayed to be a mechanism that merely processes information. Individuals are not believed to be actively involved in creating their environment, but only to respond to input. Additionally, logic is assumed to be universal, and is understood to represent the ability to deduce conclusions from higher-order principles. Again, the element of interpretation is deemed unimportant; the basis of logic is unquestioned and deduction remains unaffected by cultural differences. Norms are thus presumed to be ahistorical, or unaffected by local considerations. Normal persons, simply stated, are rational, which is a determination that is made according to technical guidelines. As a result, intervention may be transformed gradually to the point that simple technical fixes are proposed to solve problems. The utility of certain social arrangements may never be given serious consideration, for investigating the social system requires the exercise of values. And typically, technocrats strive to be value-free, or try to conceal the motives for their actions.

The most important problem with the computer microworld is that it comes into direct conflict with the philosophy that inspired the Community Mental Health Centers Act of 1963. Subsequent to the passage of this legislation, the delivery of social services is supposed to be "community based." Community based intervention, in short, is supposed to be socially sensitive and geared to the settings in which problems are thought to exist. Social sensitivity is the cornerstone of what President Kennedy referred to as his "bold new approach" to addressing mental health issues.[45] Correspondingly, standardization was supposed to be replaced by a more appropriate method for making decisions about clients. But if practitioners are not careful, the current desire to computerize social service agencies may result in the spirit of the Community Mental Health Centers Act being violated.

The surreptitious operation of the computer microworld may implode the perception of practitioners to the extent that the social character of intervention prescribed by the Community Mental Health Act is lost. For example, clinicians are supposed to be their clients' advocates. But if intervention becomes simply a technical undertaking, this sort of activism may be viewed as passé. What must be remembered is that effective practitioners are not technicians, but agents of change. As such, intervention must be guided by principles that are not necessarily technical. In this respect, altering a client's life should not be explained by algorithms or other abstract formulae. Contextual, personal, and interpersonal considerations should not be ignored. Yet these phenomena are not easily defined or readily computerized. Consequently, in the Computer Age, they may come to be treated as ancillary to proposing a sound intervention. Nonetheless, the lure of computerization must never become so great that this travesty is allowed to occur.

## NOTES

1. Margaret Boden, *Artificial Intelligence and Natural Man* (New York: Basic Books, 1977), pp. 15-17.

2. J. David, Bolter, *Turing's Man: Western Culture in the Computer Age* (Chapel Hill: University of North Carolina Press, 1984).

3. Thomas S. Kuhn, *The Structure of Scientific Revolutions* (Chicago: University of Chicago Press, 1962).

4. Bolter, *Turing's Man*, pp. 83-90.

5. Dreyfus and Dreyfus, *Mind over Machine*, p. 54.

6. Lyotard, *The Postmodern Condition*, p. 86.

7. Felix Guattari, *The Molecular Revolution* (New York: Penguin Books, 1984), pp. 87, 163.

8. Terry Winograd, "Artificial Intelligence and Language Comprehension," in *Artificial Intelligence and Language Comprehension* (Washington, DC: National Institute of Education, 1976), p. 9.

9. Lyotard, *The Postmodern Condition*, p. 4.

10. Dreyfus and Dreyfus, *Mind over Machine*, p. 53.

11. S. G. Shanker, "AI at the Crossroads," in *The Question of Artificial*

*Intelligence*, ed. Brian P. Bloomfield (London: Croom Helm, 1987), pp. 1-58.

12. Herbert L. Dreyfus, *What Computers Can't Do* (New York: Harper and Row, 1972), p. 77.

13. Theodore Roszak, *The Cult of Information* (New York: Pantheon Books, 1986), p. 120.

14. John W. Murphy and John T. Pardeck, "Technology in Clinical Practice and the Technological Ethic," *Journal of Sociology and Social Welfare*, 15(1) (1988): pp. 119-128.

15. John W. Murphy, "The Importance of Schutz's Phenomenology for Computerization," in *Worldly Phenomenology*, ed. Lester Embree (Washington, D.C: University Press of America, 1988), pp. 137-149.

16. Dreyfus and Dreyfus, *Mind over Machine*, p. 63.

17. Gilles Deleuze and Felix Guattari, *On the Line* (New York: Semiotext(e), 1983), p. 90.

18. Dreyfus and Dreyfus, *Mind over Machine*, p. 203.

19. Herbert Marcuse, *One-Dimensional Man* (Boston: Beacon Press, 1964), pp. 1-18.

20. Niklas Luhmann, *The Differentiation of Society* (New York: Columbia University Press, 1982), pp. 353-355.

21. William Barrett, *The Illusion of Technique* (Garden City, NY: Anchor Press, 1978), p. 37.

22. Vernon Pratt, *Thinking Machines* (Oxford: Basil Blackwell, 1987), pp. 45-69.

23. Murad D. Akhundov, *Conceptions of Space and Time* (Cambridge: MIT Press, 1986), p. 95.

24. Adolf Grünbaum, *Philosophical Problems of Space and Time* (Dordrecht: D. Reidel, 1973), pp. 4-8.

25. Pratt, *Thinking Machines*, pp. 48-56.

26. Dreyfus, *What Computers Can't Do*, pp. 70-75.

27. Robert Brown, *The Nature of Social Laws* (Cambridge: Cambridge University Press, 1984), pp. 49-69

28. Pratt, *Thinking Machines*, p. 70.

29. Ibid., pp. 126-135.

30. Dreyfus and Dreyfus, *Mind over Machine*, pp. 189-201.

31. *New York Times*, 29 March 1984.

32. Dreyfus and Dreyfus, *Mind over Machine*, pp. 101ff.

33. Edward Feigenbaum and Pamela McCorduck, *The Fifth Generation: Artificial Intelligence and Japan's Computer Challenge to the World* (Lexington, MA: Addison-Wesley, 1983), p. 38

34. Dreyfus and Dreyfus, *Mind over Machine*, p. 76.

35. Roger Schank, and Robert Abelson, *Scripts, Plans, Goals, and Un-*

*derstanding* (Hillsdale, NJ: Lawrence Erlbaum Associates, 1977), pp. 36-68.

36. Terry Winograd, "A Procedural Model of Language Understanding," in *Computer Models of Thought and Language*, ed. Roger C. Schank and Kenneth Mark Colby (San Francisco: W. H. Freeman and Co., 1973), pp. 152-186.

37. Dreyfus and Dreyfus, *Mind over Machine*, pp. 101-121.

38. Dreyfus, *What Computers Can't Do*, pp. 159-224.

39. Herbert A. Simon, *The Sciences of the Artificial* (Cambridge, 2nd ed.: MIT Press, 1981), pp. 24-25.

40. Dreyfus, *What Computers Can't Do*, p. 206.

41. Daniel Dennett, "Cognitive Wheels: The Frame Problem of AI," in *Minds, Machines, and Evolution*, ed. Christopher Hookway (Cambridge: Cambridge University Press, 1984), pp. 129-151.

42. Winograd and Flores, *Understanding Computers and Cognition*, p. 133.

43. Dreyfus and Dreyfus, *Mind over Machine*, pp. 16-51.

44. Bolter, *Turing's Man*, p. 14.

45. David Ingleby, "Understanding Mental Illness," in *Critical Psychiatry*, ed. David Ingleby (New York: Pantheon Books, 1980), pp. 23-71.

# 3

---

# Rationalizing the Organization

Social services agencies are becoming increasingly more complex and multifaceted as they respond to the changing needs of society. Administrative personnel have attempted to adjust to the new demands placed on them by implementing the latest computer technology. But, as a result of these new technologies, the delivery of services is becoming thoroughly rationalized.

In order for computer technology to be used effectively in a human service program, an agency's activities must be translated into the language of computers. This means that many of the functions performed by workers and administrative personnel must be quantified. This approach to service delivery results in many of the traditional activities conducted by practitioners being conceptualized in extremely limited terms.[1] Obviously, some aspects of social intervention do not lend themselves well to computerization, and these activities are gradually eliminated or conducted in the traditional fashion. Most problematic, in terms of the treatment process, the nonquantifiable aspects of social intervention may simply be omitted from the clinical record. Thus a significant percentage of service activities may never be recorded or understood properly by those concerned with the accountability of practitioners or administrators. Research suggests that clinicians may become complacent and limit their search behavior, as a result of computerizing interview schedules.[2]

Numerous social practitioners reject the notion that practice can be quantified.[3] Central to this argument is that most aspects of the helping process are so intuitive that they cannot be translated readily into the language of computers.[4] An example of this is the difficulty of transforming into quantifiable terms the feeling a practitioner has when he or she has established a positive relationship with a client. Obviously, some concrete indices of this phenomenon can be identified, such as a client arriving for appointments on time or becoming verbal during the treatment sessions. But, the way a worker recognizes such a positive relationship is difficult to measure with respect to precise quantitative indicators. As suggested earlier, this rationalization of the intervention process is demanded by computer technology; that is, treatment must be reduced to the logic of computerization.

Keeping the above issues in mind, the following presents a sample of the ways in which computer technology is being used in agencies. One must keep in mind that the organization of the human service agency is transformed significantly as a result of this trend toward increased computerization.


## A BRIEF DESCRIPTION OF A MICROCOMPUTER SYSTEM

The microcomputer has become the most popular technology for regulating organizational activities. The microcomputer, in turn, can easily be linked to a larger mainframe system. Among other things, this link allows workers to communicate with each other through their individual microcomputers.

The advantage of a microcomputer work station is that large amounts of information can be handled quickly and efficiently without having to leave the office. Like the mainframe system, the microcomputer is composed basically of four systems: an input device, storage devices, a central processing unit, and an output device. Additionally, software packages facilitate communication between the various parts of the system. Numerous software packages are available to perform a multitude of functions and address a total range of human services needs, ranging from managerial procedures to complex clinical activities.

A user normally enters data into the computer through a keyboard similar to that found on a typewriter. For larger computer systems, computer cards or tapes may be used as input devices. The storage medium for the microcomputer is usually the disk. Disks allow the user to store an almost infinite amount of data. The many software packages available on disk help the user perform a host of activities that support the work process. Key organizational activities can be facilitated in this way: inventory testing, word processing, and recording.

## Inventory Testing

A variety of software packages are available to help a practitioner document and assess the presenting problems of individual clients. For example, the Minnesota Multiphasic Personality Inventory (MMPI) can be administered and scored using a microcomputer. Although some practitioners doubt the validity of this procedure, users routinely report that clients often accept automated testing over paper-and-pencil administered inventories.[5] Since the processing of inventories and automated tests can be accomplished precisely and rapidly, feedback can be provided to practitioners and clients almost instantly.

## Word Processing

Many software packages are available that enable users to create and edit documents, as well as print them. Clearly, this option allows for better record keeping, as case records can be neatly recorded, easily stored, and put into a standardized format. Other typical uses of word processing are for writing letters and producing reports.[6]

Advanced editing and typing functions, such as correcting errors and making deletions, can be performed with several simple keystrokes. The advantage of word processing is that a client's progress can be documented on a disk, and treatment plans and management reports can be generated with little effort. Clearly, word processing can facilitate many of the organizational and clinical activities required to maintain an office.

## Recording

A critical component of the treatment process is documenting, monitoring, and recording assessment and intervention efforts. Software programs are now available that can conduct a psychosocial interview and record the results of this important clinical process. These automated interviews, as they are sometimes called, follow fixed-format protocol, and thus have been evaluated to be more comprehensive than open-ended or free-flowing approaches.[7] During in-take evaluations, pressures are often present that result in social practitioners forgetting information or not asking particular questions. The type of format utilized by computerized interviews, which direct the monitoring, documenting, and recording of information, are designed to prevent the kind of omissions that can make a record sloppy, incomplete, and inaccurate. One liability is that increased rigor may be gained at the expense of flexibility.[8]

If the number of clients is great, reviewing treatment plans can be very time consuming and difficult to organize. But treatment plans based on goal attainment scaling, for instance, can be easily computerized, since treatment goals and objectives are precisely defined in measurable terms.[9] Also, a timetable can be developed that indicates when a plan needs to be reviewed next, thereby developing an automatic review schedule. In addition to treatment plans, software packages have been created for standardizing medical and counseling records. Negative citations by funding agencies can be avoided by allowing these files to be checked by a computer for omissions and errors. Before records can be evaluated in this manner, however, they must be structured according to a fixed format.[10]

## MANAGEMENT FUNCTIONS

The management information system (MIS) is the main device currently used to computerize the majority of agency functions. To guarantee the effectiveness of a MIS, the design must be compatible with cognate agencies. For example, if an information system is being installed in a mental health agency, the data collected should be pertinent to other relevant service providers, not to mention all funders. Wordarski suggests one way to accomplish this goal is to have yearly evaluations of the information that is collected and exchanged between agencies. The thrust of this evaluation should be to ascertain how other human services professionals use the information, the types of data collected, and how the organization should be designed to facilitate the use of the data.[11]

Wordarski feels the following kinds of questions should be asked: What type of data is needed? What kind of software is required? What forms will be required to collect the data? How will the data be stored? If there are tremendous differences between information systems, service delivery will break down, thus creating a difficult situation for clients.[12]

The core data collected by any agency should focus on clients, workers, treatment outcomes, and the processes critical to service delivery. This information should allow managers to view immediately how clients are served, the types of services that are provided, and the quality of treatment that is offered. This critical output allows agencies to conduct other important activities that are essential to the accountability process, such as cost-benefit analysis.

When designing an information system, files are normally in a free-form or fixed-format. Free-form is often adopted to record a client's assessment, treatment, and follow up. This strategy allows personnel to describe clinical activities in great detail. However, the data that are gathered are often difficult to summarize and condense.

On the other hand, the practitioner is guided by exact parameters when a fixed-format methodology is used to generate data. This may be accomplished through a structured interview schedule that is designed, for example, to secure descriptive information about clients. Accordingly, the number of clients served, their age, income, marital status, and other important facts can be quickly summarized. Obviously, the qualitative side of treatment does not easily translate into such a fixed-format record.[13]

Before an agency institutes an information system, all agency personnel should be involved in its development. This participation will help build understanding on their part, and thus help minimize opposition to the implementation of a system. Murphy and Pardeck suggest the following non-technical issues should be considered to foster the successful development and growth of an information system:[14]

1. Understand clearly the management philosophy.
2. Identify key decision makers and the types of decisions that will have to be made.
3. Locate vital sources of information and determine the most appropriate ways to gather this data.
4. Calculate the effort needed to garner relevant information in a socially sensitive manner.
5. Attempt to integrate conceptual, logistical, and social considerations.
6. Determine the social character of relevant data.
7. Know the culture of an organization, so that the information will flow smoothly from place to place.
8. Appreciate how the conceptual side of MIS development can enhance research and other activities.
9. Use a MIS project as an opportunity to integrate an organization.

It must be noted that there are no shortcuts to properly developing an information system. An agency should not rush into this process: both the technical and nontechnical aspects of MIS creation should receive attention.

As might be suspected, the managerial applications of an information system are extensive. In addition to documenting and organizing data related to client services, managers have found that computers can be tremendous time-savers in generating personnel and payroll reports. In short, computer technology enables an agency to monitor activities in ways that were impossible in the past, without extreme effort.

As managers and workers realize, an inordinate amount of time and energy in traditional social service agencies is beginning to be devoted to paperwork. A MIS can significantly reduce the amount of paperwork, as a result of producing and storing data mechanically rather than manually. This strategy is far more cost-effective and efficient than traditional means. For example, an efficient information system can dramatically improve billing and financial screening practices, review and revision of fee schedules, and maintenance of operating accounts and reserves to reduce cash flow problems.[15]

## ORGANIZING PROGRAM EVALUATION

Modern day computer technology has revolutionized the way agencies conduct research and undertake program evaluation. A few years ago, computer applications in human services were extremely limited and were largely used for only accounting and a very restrictive range of record keeping. By the late 1980s, however, the microcomputer enabled agencies to conduct numerous kinds of routine research.[16]

The traditional use of the computer in program evaluation has been to assist in coding and describing data. But now microcomputer software packages allow almost all agency personnel to conduct advanced statistical analyses, such as multiple regression and factor analysis. In the past, this kind of advanced multivariate analysis could only be conducted by consultants on a mainframe computer system. Furthermore, software packages currently available to human services agencies can help select a sample for data analysis, as well as implement experimental and quasi-experimental designs on a large scale.

Other important research activities that can be enhanced through the use of computer technology relate to conducting literature reviews, illustrating findings in the form of charts and graphs, and allowing input to be manipulated in an almost unlimited number of ways.[17]

### Computers in Administering Outcome Measures

A critical aspect of program evaluation is the determination of treatment outcome. In the past, formal assessment consisted largely of paper-and-pencil devices that were completed by the client and scored by a practitioner. Over the past few years, a growing number of these clinical scales have been computerized. Putting scales into a computerized format means that they are less cumbersome and disruptive to both clients and organizational routines.

The computerized interview is another recent development. It not only facilitates intervention but also clearly assists practitioners in evaluating the effect of treatment. Erdman and his colleagues note, "in contrast to human-administered interviews, computer interviews are 100 percent reliable; computers never forget to ask a question, and given the same pattern of responses by a client, the computer will always ask the same questions in the same way."[18] Such standardization allows for comparisons to be made between clinical cases, thereby promoting the adoption of increasingly sophisticated strategies to assess outcome.

In terms of research, collecting sensitive information from clients may be easier through the use of computers. Oftentimes clients will be more apt to divulge sensitive information to a computer than a fellow human being. Colby summarized the advantages of the computer in this way: "It (the computer) does not get tired, angry, or bored. It is always willing to listen and to give evidence of being heard. It can work at any time of the day or night, every day of the week, every month of the year. It does not have family problems of its own. It never gets sick or hung over. Its performance does not vary from hour to hour or from day to day."[19]

Clearly, with regard to conducting program evaluation, Colby's remarks suggest the reliability of research is enhanced, although this finding has not been confirmed in every study.[20] Furthermore, computer-administered questions can increase the integrity of data as a result of eliminating incomplete responses, for the attention of clients is directed to items that are overlooked. As most individuals involved in program evaluation and other forms of social research will testify, the problem of missing data is a major methodological issue that must be addressed.

Furthermore, new software packages are available that allow the progress of treatment to be assessed through direct interaction with a client. This form of evaluation is based on the single-subject (N = 1) methodology, a quasi-experimental design. Emphasized by this procedure is the continuous or nearly continuous measurement of a dependent variable on a single-research subject over a time interval that is divided into a baseline phase and one or more additional periods when the independent variable is manipulated. The power of this design is derived from statistical analysis, which in turn helps clinicians to decide whether a treatment is working or not.

At this time, the use of spreadsheets in conjunction with the single-subject design has become quite popular. With the spreadsheet the researcher can graph data neatly and do an array of statistical evaluations. The term *spreadsheet* originated from an accounting system for organizing financial data on special grids of rows and columns. Even though accounting applications were the impetus for spreadsheets, practitioners have discovered many different uses for the program. In particular, as described below, single-subject research has proliferated due to this innovation.

Computer Assisted Practice Evaluation (CAPE), developed by Bronson and Blythe, demonstrates how the spreadsheet can be applied to the single-subject design. CAPE is based on the LOTUS 1–2–3 program, which is currently one the most commonly used spreadsheets. To use CAPE, only basic knowledge of spreadsheet design is required, because all of the complicated steps are built into the program.[21]

CAPE allows a practitioner to use the statistical techniques that are critical to implementing the single-subject design. At the heart of CAPE is a template, which contains all the necessary formulas and explanatory labels but no data. Once the template is made operational a practitioner simply enters the data from a given single-subject experiment. This input is plotted automatically on a graph and the statistical tests selected from a menu of options are performed.

Since CAPE is easy to use, treatment does not have to be terminated before evaluating a client's performance. Baseline data can be inputed as they are received, a printed graph can be produced, and this visual image can be used in assessing or altering an intervention. As treatment proceeds, additional data can be included and statistically analyzed.

Another software package that incorporates the single-subject design is the Clinical Assessment System (CAS) developed by Hudson.[22] The CAS is a compilation of all of Hudson's scales. Each one can be used in a single-subject format. Through the use of CAS, the following items can be measured:

- depression
- self-esteem
- marital discord
- sexual discord

- parent-child relationships as seen by the parent
- mother-child relationship as seen by the child
- father-child relationship as seen by the child
- intrafamilial stress and
- peer relationships

Newer scales have been developed which assess

- personal stress
- anxiety
- alcohol abuse
- sexual attitudes
- homophobia
- partner abuse (nonphysical)
- partner abuse (physical) and
- peer relations.[23]

Also provided by CAS are graphs for visual analysis. The system is designed in such a way that a client can complete the computerized scales on a regular basis and, in turn, monitor his or her progress.

As CAPE and CAS are improved and additional packages are created to help practitioners use the single-subject design, more and more agencies will likely use this new technology. Agencies who have access to programs such as LOTUS 1–2–3 will experience little additional expense when adding the CAPE system to their repertoire. Furthermore, the CAS program not only permits single-subject evaluation but opens the door to using the computer as part of more extensive evaluation practices.

Clearly, computers are essential for undertaking research and program evaluation. The development of the microcomputer simplified calculations that were at one time very complicated and difficult. Transforming data, graphing client goals, and altering data for further analysis are mundane activities for the microcomputer. For example, the frequently used Statistical Package for the Social Sciences (SPSS) and other statistical packages are now available for use with the microcomputer. Consequently, the ability to analyze a variety of clinical phenomena is enhanced. In summary, Wordarski notes that human services agencies can effectively use computers in program evaluation to accomplish the following tasks:[24]

1. Administration and scoring tests
2. Interpretation
   Wechsler
   Rorschach
   MMPI (Minnesota Multiphasic Personality Inventory)
3. Client program planning and calculations
   goals
   case progress
   intervention plan
   timetable
4. Program documentation
   data recording and illustration
   data analysis
   attainment of legal and administrative requirements
5. Research application
   client progress
   calculations
   transformation of data
   graphing client and administrative variables
   updating information in a data base

## CONCLUSION

In this chapter, numerous ways computers can enhance organizational analysis have been presented. However, even though computerization appears to increase the efficiency and effectiveness of an agency, a number of key points must be raised about the implications of this technology for service delivery. These points relate to Weber's and, more recently, Claude Lefort's argument that the more rationalized an organization becomes, the further it is removed from the social world. Further, as emphasized by Murphy and Pardeck, even though computerization may create the illusion of objectivity and rationality within the organization, the data collected on clients may not result in useful information for social intervention.[25] In fact, much of this information may simply be irrelevant to the workings of the social world of clients and the larger community. Therefore, the general impetus for this increasing rationalization must be appreciated.

Another name for this increasing rationalization is *bureaucratization*. Indeed, most organizations in today's society are bureaucracies. And to no one's surprise, social service agencies are no exception. Over the last decade the electorate has been informed of this finding by most politicians. The sad fact is that most programs have succumbed to this trend, and thus service delivery has been negatively affected.

As Weber describes, bureaucracies appear initially to be efficient.[26] Clearly defined job descriptions are evident, along with explicit lines of authority. Accordingly, interpersonal relations become impersonal as procedural rigor is introduced into an organization. Decisions are not haphazard, because standardized criteria are available for making judgements. Formalizing an organization in this way has been assumed traditionally to culminate in improved efficiency and effectiveness. The question that must be raised at this juncture is: Will this illusion be perpetuated through the increased use of computers by practitioners?

What do persons find so appealing about bureaucracies, at least initially? As Lefort writes, the "ahistorical" culture that exists within bureaucracies has some advantages.[27] With the influence of human element minimized, idiosyncracies and other sources of bias are allegedly purged from an organization. Fairness and justice are thus thought to be enhanced. This is because each case is believed to be assessed solely in terms of its merits, for only facts can be introduced into the deliberation process.

In this sense, bureaucracy represents an attempt to make organizations function in a scientific manner. Due to the introduction of a host of procedures, individual volition is restricted. In fact, this sort of interpretation is thought to undermine reason and cause errors in judgement. According to Weber, through bureaucratization values are eliminated from organizational activities.

Yet, as Weber also recognizes, this last statement is inaccurate.[28] That is, all values are discredited except those associated with the process of bureaucratization. As a result, bureaucrats tend to focus inward and become oblivious to the social world. After all, anything other than bureaucratic standards is deemed to be corrupted by opinion, and thus serious attention should not be given to these inferior views. In this sense, reality consists of nothing more than bureaucratic rules and regulations.

Yet, as most critics indicate, this obsession with formalities has dire consequences. Most important, the decisions made by bureaucrats are often uninformed, insensitive, and thus inefficient and ineffective. But what else should be expected from a type of organization where interpretation, critique, and nontechnical considerations are presumed to be anathema to rationality? As a result, the effects of bureaucratization are devastating.

Eventually bureaucracies become indifferent to nonbureaucratic values and beliefs. Actually, innovation is stifled once reason is associated with a particular format. In a social service agency, narrowing the ability of practitioners in this way is unproductive, considering the multivalent character of most clients' problems.

As should be recognized, however, bureaucracy and computerization reflect similar premises. Both are based on the unfounded principle that accuracy and efficiency are impeded by the presence of the human element. Therefore, bureaucracy will probably be enhanced by the introduction of computers, unless the proper correctives are taken. Some of these remedies are discussed in detail in chapter 4, with regard to avoiding the complete rationalization of an agency by a MIS.

Clearly, most of the technical innovations that have been generated to improve organizational analysis foster bureaucratization. Even word processing, as is discussed by Michael Heim, strips writing of its human significance.[29] "Natural language [is] interpreted as a standard code," he says. In short, writing is mechanized and simultaneously decontextualized. And when the administration of tests or program evaluation becomes simply a technical exercise, certain questions by their fundamental nature are inappropriate. Specifically, issues that may expand decision are eschewed.

In sum, computerization is consistent with a bureaucratic ethos. This association should be remembered by those who believe that the presence of computers will somehow expand the generation and use of data, especially if the managerial aim is to avoid the bureaucratization of services. But computerization fits nicely into a plan to make agencies efficient, as a consequence of streamlining activities. Such an organization, however, may prove to be very costly in the long run.

## NOTES

1. John A. Sckinka and R. Rob Smith, "The Computer in the Psychotherapist's Office: Present and Future Applications," in *Using Computers in Clinical Practice*, ed. Marc D. Schwartz (New York: The Haworth Press, 1984): pp. 7-17.

2. Mike Fitter, "The Development and Use of Information Technology in Health Care," in *Information Technology and People*, ed. Frank Blackler and David Oborne (Cambridge: MIT Press, 1987), pp. 116-117.

3. John W. Murphy and John T. Pardeck, "Technologically Mediated Therapy: A Critique," *Social Casework* 67 (10) (1986): pp. 605-612.

4. John T. Pardeck and John W. Murphy, "Microcomputer Technology in Clinical Social Work Practice: Benefits and Problems," *ARETE* 11 (1) (1986): pp. 35-43.

5. Schinka and Smith, "The Computer in the Psychotherapist's Office: Present and Future Applications," p. 10.

6. Danny Wedding, "The Word Processor as a Patient Education Tool in Psychotherapy," in *Using Computers in Clinical Practice*, ed. Marc D. Schwartz (New York: The Haworth Press, 1984), pp. 381-382.

7. A. C. Carr, A. Ghosh, and R. J. Ancill, "Can a Computer Take a Psychiatric History?" *Psychological Medicine*, 13(1) (1983): pp. 151-158; Hugh V. Angle, "The Interviewing Computer: A Technology for Gathering Comprehensive Information," *Behavior Research Methods and Instrumentation*, 13(4) (1981): pp. 607-612.

8. Fitter, "The Development and Use of Information Technology in Health Care," p. 120.

9. Thomas J. Kiresuk and Sander H. Lund, "Process and Outcome Measurement Using Goal Attainment Scaling," in *Program Evaluation: Alcohol, Drug, and Mental Health Services*, ed. Jack Zussman and Cecil R. Wurster (Lexington, MA: Lexington Books, 1975), pp. 213-228.

10. Wesley L. Nolden, "Technology and Transference: Computers in Psychotherapy," in *Technology and Human Productivity: Challenges for the Future*, ed. John W. Murphy and John T. Pardeck (Westport, CT: Greenwood Press, 1986), pp. 67-75.

11. John S. Wodarski, "Development of Management Information Systems for Human Services: A Practical Guide," *Computer in Human Services* 3 (1 and 2) (1988): pp. 37-49.

12. Ibid.

13. John W. Murphy and John T. Pardeck, "Important Non-Technical Considerations in the Development of an MI System," in *Computers in Human Services: An Overview for Clinical and Welfare Services*, ed. John T. Pardeck and John W. Murphy (London: Harwood Academic Publishers, 1990), pp. 129-136.

14. Ibid, p. 130.

15. Wodarski, "Development of Management Information Systems for Human Services: A Practical Guide," pp. 37-49.

16. Ibid.

17. Dvane R. Monette, Thomas J. Sullivan, and Cornell R. DeJong, *Applied Social Research: Tool for the Human Services*, 2nd ed. (New York: Holt, Rinehart and Winston, Inc., 1990).

18. Harold P. Erdman, M. H. Klein, and John H. Greist, "Direct Patient Computer Interviewing," *Journal of Consulting and Clinical Psychology* 53(6) (1985): pp. 760-773.

19. Kenneth M. Colby, "Computer Psychotherapists," in *Technology in Mental Health Care Delivery Systems*, ed. Joseph B. Sidowsk, James H. Johnson, and Thomas A. Williams (Norwood, NJ: Ablex, 1980), p. 14.

20. Fitter "The Development and Use of Information Technology in Health Care," p. 120.

21. D. E. Bronson and B. J. Blythe, "Computer Support for Single-Case Evaluation of Practice," *Social Work Research and Abstracts* (23) (1987): pp. 10-13.

22. Walter W. Hudson, *CAS: The Clinical Assessment System* (Tallahassee, FL: WALMYR Publishing Co., 1988).

23. Walter W. Hudson and Paula S. Nurius, *Computer Assisted Practice: Theory, Methods, and Software* (Belmont, CA: Wadsworth Publishing Company, 1991).

24. Wodarski, "Development of Management Information Systems for Human Services: A Practical Guide," pp. 42-43.

25. Murphy and Pardeck, "Nontechnical Correctives for High-Tech Systems in Social Service Agencies," pp. 63-73; Murphy, Pardeck, Nolden, and Pilotta, "Conceptual Issues Related to the Use of Computers in Social Work Practice," pp. 63-73.

26. Max Weber, *Economy and Society*, vol. II (Berkeley: University of California Press, 1978), pp. 956-958.

27. Claude Lefort, *The Political Forms of Modern Society* (Cambridge: MIT Press, 1986), p. 222.

28. Weber, *Economy and Society*, pp. 996-991.

29. Michael Heim, *Electric Language: A Philosophical Study of Word Processing* (New Haven: Yale University Press, 1987), p. 82.

# 4

---

# MIS Development and
# Organizational Culture

## INTRODUCTION

As noted in the previous chapter, management information systems
(MIS) have become a vital part of most social service agencies. And
with the proliferation of all sorts of hardware and software, computerized information systems have become almost commonplace.
Indeed, the survivability of an agency is now often linked to the
successful deployment of a MIS.[1] If an office is disorganized, and
thus inefficient, the installation of a MIS is thought to remedy this
problem. Also, a MIS will supposedly enhance decision making, as
a result of supplying a managerial support function. In short, the
belief is prevalent that whatever ails an organization can be cured
by a MIS. A MIS has almost a magical quality, not unlike computers,
with respect to the majority of agency personnel.

Minus the hyperbole, what is the purpose of a MIS? What can
reasonably be expected from these devices? Minimally, a MIS is
designed to identify, channel, store, and generate information upon
request.[2] Considering the argument in chapter 1, implementing and
utilizing a MIS should not be viewed simply as a technical exercise.
Identifying and channeling knowledge, for example, are obviously
communicative processes. Yet most often MIS development is ap-

proached as a primarily technological undertaking. Given the persuasiveness of the technological world-view, this charge should not be surprising. Nonetheless, a MIS does have profound social implications. More may be affected, in other words, than merely the technical and organizational skills of workers.

The claim is made in this chapter that the entire culture of an agency can be altered by a MIS.[3] In order to appreciate this argument, readers must recognize that organizations are not simply inanimate objects comprised of rules, structures, work flows, and hierarchies. This point will be explored in more detail later on in this chapter. For right now, however, the idea that agencies operate according to specific assumptions about knowledge, order, and decorum is most important. These presuppositions outline behavioral expectations, along with the procedures that are accepted as typical for coping with difficulties and completing work. Moreover, these so-called informal standards are often vital to promoting the human side of work. The morale and productivity of workers are tied intimately to the culture of an organization, argue many modern writers.[4]

With the onset of a MIS, the ways in which agency personnel view themselves, their jobs, and their relationships to fellow workers may be irremediably altered. Violating the culture of an organization in this way, accordingly, may foster alienation. The insight workers have gained from solving problems and resolving interpersonal conflicts may be lost. This valuable knowledge may be dismissed as insignificant, because primacy is given to technical operations. Further, the values, beliefs, and commitments that bind persons together may be destroyed. Overlooked, in short, may be the key aspects of work that are interpersonally negotiated. These elements, nonetheless, provide an organization with its character. An organization's culture is not necessarily obtrusive, but is related inextricably to layers of personal and collective experiences.

The changes that may be brought about in an agency by a MIS stem from the computer microworld. To be specific, imagery that may have deleterious consequences is advanced about knowledge, communication, organizational integration, and information. Not unexpectedly, these factors of organizational life are thoroughly formalized when they are associated with technological rationality. Unfortunately, rarefied notions about the identification, dissemination, and utilization of information may come to undermine an agency, for how these tasks are actually undertaken on a daily basis may be obscured. Organizational culture is thus subverted by what is perceived to be a foreign reality.

Most important at this juncture is what happens when structural metaphors are adopted to describe an organization. Reinforcing the structure, noting current and potential breaks, and proposing structurally sound remedies that enhance information flow is the job of a MIS. Also suggested by this imagery is that clear, precise, and neatly packaged information is what decision makers need. Therefore, information that meets the specifications set by the structural imperatives of an organization is given a high priority. What this suggests is that the mechanization of knowledge is pursued.

Accordingly, management and other key operations of an agency are supposed to be improved following the implementation of a MIS, for disorganization is thought to be remedied. The fragmentation and lack of direction that will spell the demise of an organization are assumed to be brought to an end by the use of a MIS. Through the routinization of activities, regularity, certainty, and a comprehensive outlook can be achieved.[5] As a result of a systemic approach to organizing data, precision and order are gained. Yet how are these goals achieved?

## DEVELOPING A MIS

When inaugurating a MIS, the first step is to locate sources of information. In a manner of speaking, these locations constitute subsystems within the overall organization. These modules will most often be departments, although smaller components may be used. Most important at this juncture is that uniform reporting requirements be established. Milano, for example, refers to this activity as introducing "data discipline."[6] Information must no longer be esoteric, or defined solely by individual department heads. Stressing uniformity implies that data have a role to play in maintaining the entire organization. Thus data must be decontextualized, for as Kanter states, the use of "local rationality" is unproductive.[7]

Next the flow of information must be conceptualized. The point is that knowledge does not stay in one place, but moves throughout an organization. Data must move from the periphery of an organization to its center in the most efficient manner possible. The flow of knowledge, in other words, must be structured. Standard flow diagramming techniques are usually implemented for this purpose. For example, information may follow clients or the authority structure in an agency. In either case, however, knowledge must be prepared for its trip. Milano calls this "information discipline."[8] Information, stated differently, must become increasingly abstract, in order to have relevance on the various stops along the transmittal path. Remember that, eventually, data are going to be used by high-level managers to make decisions. Information that does not fulfill the requirements of this destiny will never complete the entire journey throughout an organization. Hence data must be related explicitly to organizational goals.

The termination point of the information flow is a data base. This source of information is categorically distinct from the subcomponents of this system. Vital at this juncture is the theme of integration. Disparate pieces of information are not supposed to be simply deposited at a central site. Instead, various types of information are supposed to relate to one another. Data are integrated when they form a cohesive picture of the organization. The expectation is that data will be merged, and in this way the data base can serve as a type of organizational command center. As a result of merging data categories, comparisons can be made across all levels of an organization. Monitoring capability is thus practically unlimited at this stage of development.

An integrated, centralized data base does not, however, necessarily represent the most technically advanced product. In terms of the three phases discussed thus far, all that has been addressed is the routine collection of information. Data that are regularly gathered can be easily systematized. But what about unusual information requests? How are these demands supposed to be met? The highest stage of MIS development, therefore, relates to the ability to answer unplanned questions. A system must not only be integrated, but flexible enough to merge data categories that were not originally thought to belong together. Yet because new data cannot be added instantaneously to an information base, a MIS must be capable of achieving new levels of abstraction. Novel data categories must be created out of old ones. Flexibility is thus very important.

A high cost is incurred for establishing an integrated information base in this way. Particularly noteworthy is that data must be removed from their natural setting and become increasingly abstract. Talcott Parsons identified this movement with regard to legitimizing norms, although the principle is the same in terms of building a knowledge base.[9] Specifically, expanding the relevance of information is thought to be achieved by gradually broadening data categories, as a result of designing them to reflect universals instead of particulars. Hence conceptual breadth is achieved, while relevance may be sacrificed. This is a trade-off that will become important later on in this discussion. Particularly, contends Dery, due to the pervasiveness of technical imagery relevance is often lost and "data handling activities are controlled rather than managed."[10] Data and the flow of information are simply constrained.

However, implementing a MIS should be viewed as a social process, despite the claims made by experts in systems design. Obviously, agreeing on definitions of knowledge, communicating, establishing information networks, and gaining access to local and organizational data bases are all involved in this activity. As might be suspected, problems begin to arise when technological (structural) imagery is used to identify knowledge and integrate this information to form a comprehensive data base. Increasing abstraction is justified, even encouraged, while the culture of an organization is deanimated. Nonetheless, the acquisition and utilization of information are thought to be improved. Increased efficiency is believed to culminate in the collection of better data and more effective management.

## CYBERNETIC IMAGERY AND CULTURE

Cybernetics, also known as information theory, represents a breakthrough in explaining events and is usually tied to the development of a MIS. A new model has emerged, wherein energy is replaced by information. Many benefits are thought to be derived from this novel mode of conceptualization. Whereas energy is a somewhat vague notion, information is not. Additionally, suggested by the notion of information is that knowledge can be controlled, given explicit direction, altered systematically, and refined through trial and error. Through the introduction of concepts such as coding, storage, noise, feedback, etc., the old ways of thinking about the acquisition and diffusion of knowledge have been changed forever.[11] As a consequence of cybernetics, the random distribution of energy no longer serves as the only rational explanation of events. Now, matter or, in more social terms, stimuli can be viewed as regulated, rather than impinging randomly on a blank slate or physiological receptors. In a manner of speaking, data can be thought to have a purpose, rather than simply consisting of raw material.

In terms of life within an organization, this shift in viewpoint means that institutions should not be considered natural systems. Rather than believing organizations have natural tendencies to develop, these agencies can be managed. In fact, the rationale for instituting a MIS is sustained by this change in outlook. Organizations are no longer to be understood as guided by a *telos*, evolutionary tendencies, or other nebulous principles. Instead, control can now be systematically imposed. Yet the question still remains: What is the cost of this control? As suggested earlier in this chapter, through the use of cybernetic imagery the culture of an organization may be transformed into something that is barely recognizable. The point is that a cybernetic environment may gradually become inhospitable, as is claimed by Lyotard.[12] A cybernetic culture may be truly artificial.

### Knowledge

Central to the operation of a cybernetic system is that knowledge becomes *information*. This is not simply a change in terminology. Metaphysics or speculation is abandoned in order to provide knowledge with exact parameters. Epistemological issues are resolved by defining knowledge in quantitative terms. Information is thus in a state that must be allowed to migrate throughout an organization.[13] Moreover, semantic problems are solved by equating meaning with difference in size: a specific quantitative measure differentiates one message from another.[14] Consequently, information is rendered exact. This maneuver is accomplished when designing a MIS by removing knowledge from its natural setting and establishing a standardized input format. Confounding factors are thus expurgated from the identification of data. Hence, data consist of entities that any rational person can observe. Facts are rendered substantial.

## Communication

The transmission of knowledge is essential to both a cybernetic system and a MIS. This sort of activity, however, is equated with information exchange in the case of cybernetics. In other words, communication is comprised of sending and receiving input, which is regularly understood to consist of stimuli. Furthermore, dialogue is known to reflect a stimulus history. This idea was pioneered by Shannon, and later improved by Weaver and Wiener. As described by Thayer, communication can be envisioned as "$A \rightarrow M \rightarrow B = X$."[15] What this means is that a sender (A) sends a message (M) to a receiver (B), thereby producing a result (X). Streamlining communication in this way is thought to minimize unwanted interference. Linkages or transactions become almost automatic, unless interference is present. The problem is that communication is strongly suggested to be nothing more than a coded message, an array of data, and knowledge is thus decontextualized.

When establishing a MIS, systems design accomplishes this aim. In terms of operating a MIS, various forms of communication are necessary. Clear pathways are established throughout an organization, in order to insure the unencumbered transmission of data from one department to another. These channels are specified, regulated, and constantly monitored, so that access to them is limited. Therefore, information cannot be diverted or clouded by the introduction of extraneous input. What might be called undercoded data—those with inexact parameters—are eliminated from the system. Additionally, machines must communicate with each other. This is accomplished by using machine language, or metasymbols, which represents formal grammar that is purged of any syntactical ambiguities.[16] Incidentally, this mechanistic language is also given primacy when humans have to speak with machines. And finally, humans must address each other. Interpersonal relations that are mediated by a MIS are conducted in terms of standardized categories and messages. In this way, uninterrupted communication is guaranteed at several levels of the organization.

## Integration

According to cybernetic theory, integration is not a social affair. Evidence of this is found in the terms that are used to describe the construction of a knowledge base. *Nodes, modules, vectors, bubbles,* and *transactions* exemplify the language adopted to describe integration.[17] The integration of information thus becomes an exercise in engineering. Information is merged largely as a result of technical advancements, instead of cultural relevance or other social considerations. Through the creation of elaborate diagrams, typically known as a box structure, a sense of wholeness is provided.[18] Subsystems are normalized, because their respective boundaries and relationships are detailed and stabilized.

This process is undertaken as part of an overall system design. The unfortunate result, however, is that integration is equated with constructing an information net. Data base organization, therefore, is a product of insuring that the flow of information is unimpeded. Specifically, the logic of how information is arranged is instrumental in structuring the data base. The focus of integration is guaranteeing the structural integrity of pathways, removing obstacles from these networks, and insuring that the sending and receiving units are operational. In short, the logic of the system dictates how subsystems shall be related. Standards of efficiency (or instrumentality), rather than social relevance, thus begin to dominate the organization of information.

Anyone who has lived through the installation of a MIS should recognize what is being said. Often the flow chart of the MIS is mistaken for reality.[19] As a result, the natural communication channels that are operative within an organization are made to conform to the requirements of a MIS. Hence the logistical side of a MIS outlines the patterns of relevance for structuring information flow, sources of data, and knowledge subsystems. A facade of integration is maintained, but the everyday tasks of an organization are impaired.

### Knowledge Acquisition

The focus of knowledge acquisition becomes the accumulation of increasing amounts of data. In fact, having the most current information becomes the measure of success. After all, the development of a MIS is sustained by the belief that valid knowledge will be provided in a timely manner to those who need it. Yet what principles guide this process? Readers should appreciate that the primary concern is to formalize the identification and distribution of knowledge. Key to becoming informed then is the procurement of the most advanced technology. A more efficient flow of data, more equipment, and better programs are thought to lead to well informed personnel. Michael Shallis has referred to this belief as "silicon idolatry."[20]

This view of knowledge acquisition has proven to be very problematic. With little or no concern expressed for anything but quantification and efficiency, the amount of information that circulates in organizations has proliferated.[21] This condition has been referred to by some writers as an "information glut." What else can be expected, notes Lyotard, when technical criteria underpin knowledge acquisition?[22] For questions pertaining to truth, value, and validity, for example, are only tangentially related to technical issues. As a matter of fact, some critics wonder whether managers are better informed as a result of improved MIS technology.[23] Are managers and other personnel in agencies getting information that is useful?

All that appears to have happened is that more information is available. Yet guidelines pertaining to how this knowledge should be used are often nothing more than an afterthought! Moreover, enormous competition has been spawned with regard to gaining knowledge. Sometimes various separate data bases are developed surreptitiously within an organization, with individuals hoarding information.[24] Indeed, in the Computer Age knowledge is power and thus gaining access to storage and distribution centers is a primary pursuit. And if only technical standards accompany the development of a MIS, management may not be upgraded. Actually, this undirected increase in information may only cause chaos.

The Dreyfuses maintain that this emphasis on technology has caused management skills to atrophy.[25] Analytic management, as they call it, usually overlooks the so-called soft activities that are essential to effectively operating an organization: goal formation, critical assessment of knowledge, and the ability to change perspectives rapidly. Clearly, these are value-based or experienced-based activities that are unrelated to technical improvements. Yet without a value base, knowledge has no direction, and thus information merely accumulates at an ever-increasing rate. But calculative rationality is supposed to be devoid of prescriptive elements.

The strength of a MIS, in other words, is that it is supposedly not influenced by sociological variables. If systems design is correctly undertaken, the flow of information should be efficient and reach its target audience on time. Values, in other words, may subvert this process.

### Management vs. Technocracy

But is good management a value-free enterprise? According to a host of new writers this is not the case.[26] Nowadays managers are encouraged to understand the reality of an organization, in terms of how this realm is perceived by employees. The common sense knowledge that operates at the level of the shop floor or department is considered to be a vital component in management decision making. In fact, the input of workers has been elevated significantly in this regard. Quality of working life projects, quality circles, and self-management are beginning to receive attention in many agencies. As a result, the knowledge base of managers is supposed to be expanded at every opportunity, thereby improving management activity.

Yet does the model of knowledge and reason presupposed by a MIS enlarge a data base in this way? The Dreyfuses, for example, say no.[27] Their point is that a MIS is designed to handle only hard data, that which is readily observable, quantifiable, and easily transmitted through highly structured media. In this sense, levels of information are tacitly established; priority is given to particular types of input. Equally problematic is that technical experts may come to dominate organizations, because these elaborate information systems need special attention.[28] Not every employee has the skills required to monitor or repair a MIS.

What this means is that a cybernetic orientation may culminate in a technocracy, where only technical knowledge is allowed to influence decision making and experts dominate the process of management. Such organizations are not managed but administrated. Systems analysts, simply put, are not necessarily managers. The point is that technocracies are directed by abstract forces, with little or no concern for situational exigencies. Accordingly, technocracies tend to be inhumane, which should be a matter of importance for the managers of social service agencies. For when these programs become technocracies the focus is on technique and technical train-ing, while a small cadre of experts make most of the organizational decisions. Most discussions, in short, are centered around technical issues. But burn-out should not be encouraged because of the im-agery that is adopted to conceptualize the internal environment of an organization; the basic structure of an agency should not con-tribute to persons leaving the helping professions.

## CULTURAL LIFE AFTER A MIS?

Central to this critique thus far is that organizations consist of more than jobs, patterns of authority, and lines of communication. These descriptive devices, in fact, are thought to distort what goes on inside of organizations. Institutions are not static, as is suggested by these terms. What is overlooked are the processes that serve to maintain organizational life. According to Karl Weick, for example, organizations are basically interlocking realms of symbolism.[29] In other words, organizations constitute symbols that are not questioned.

Terms such as *open, multidimensional, dynamic, flexible, fluid*, and so on, are currently used by managers who are thought to be progressive.[30] Their point is that organizations are no longer con-ceived to represent structural imperatives. In fact, structural barriers and rigid cognitive categories are assumed to prohibit growth. Joint problem solving, the intermingling of very different ideas, and suf-ficient space for experimentation, for example, are treated as es-sential to foster the entrepreneurial spirit. Tapping unexpected contributions is the overall aim of this change in organizational style.

Relative to the traditional view of organizations, this is a radical step. In short, organizations are not ominous forces, which operate according to structural or fixed laws and natural tendencies. Ac-cording to Weick, managers and other employees create the envi-ronments of organizations. Certain types of reason or rationality are thus abandoned, while others are maintained. According to one management philosophy, particular behaviors are expected, yet in terms of another these same actions are deemed bizarre. Hence organizational environments are always changing, according to a strategy of "enactment-selection-retention."[31] In other words, the reality of an organization is invented and thus quite fragile. This idea is compatible with a notion that will be discussed later on in this book: reality is not external but an outgrowth of "language games."[32] Anyway, prohibitions, limitations, and possibilities are thus dependent on ways reality is defined and enforced.

This means that organizational environments are replete with common-sense knowledge that is created and preserved through a variety of activities. For example, persons come to work with very different expectations, and as a result of subtle negotiations the protocol for dealing with issues is gradually instituted. Managers and workers must also negotiate with each other, for either party could easily sabotage the work process. As Weick states, persons enact recipes that have pragmatic importance and are used to judge whether or not a solution to a problem is adequate.[33] Hence behavioral expectations are based on a stock of knowledge that is always subject to further alteration.

Recent research suggests that key to organizational life is civility—i.e., the ability to merge goals, tolerate differences, and foster innovation—rather than information.[34] In this regard, Egon Bittner writes that "formal organizational designs are schemes of interpretation that competent and entitled users can invoke in unknown ways whenever it suites their purposes."[35] A realm of free play is thus available for employees, in terms of responding to and initiating proposals. Accordingly, cybernetic imagery is thought in many circles to be inappropriate for describing organizational life. Knowledge, communication, and integration, for instance, are seriously misconstrued as a result of the reality assumptions that underpin a MIS. Most important, the effort that must be devoted to constructing facts and avoiding misinterpretation is devalued. Instead, the focus is on the technical side of gathering and disseminating information.

As opposed to the recommendations of the technicians who build these abstract systems, facts should not be removed from their natural setting. Only from within the layers of symbolism where they reside, can the meaning of facts be appreciated. Hence removing facts from their context can be disastrous. Likewise, communication is not the same as transmitting information, for the expectations persons have play a large role in determining how knowledge is interpreted. Values, in other words, should not be severed from facts. And finally, knowledge integration has more to do with accepting and rejecting symbolism, than with joining data bases mechanically through systems design. Knowledge integration is a question of information becoming thematic, or relevant, at certain times during the operation of an organization.

What about the question of organizational life after the installation of a MIS? Surely the culture of an organization can survive a MIS. After all, technology is not indomitable. The solution is not to mistake the model for reality. Stated differently, gathering and disseminating knowledge should not be equated with one procedure or regulatory strategy. Does the operation of an MIS have to deanimate an organization? Of course not. Nonetheless, the principles that usually sustain the development of a MIS must be replaced by ones that are more socially sensitive. Rather than value-free, a MIS must be value-based. A MIS, for example, must incorporate the communication networks that are present in an organization, instead of destroying these channels. In general, the logic of a MIS should mimic the interpretive knowledge that provides the foundation for an organization's culture. Developing a MIS should not be used as an opportunity to overcome the effects of an organization's culture, as is often the case.

## STEPS TOWARD AN UNOBTRUSIVE MIS

A MIS does not have to be obtrusive and disruptive of the culture of an organization. Preserving this dimension of a social service agency, however, requires strategic planning. A holistic action plan must be formulated, one that is not restricted to dealing with technical practices. The following list is not exhaustive, but provides an expanded discussion of the recommendations that appear in chapter 3.

1. Managers should be made aware of the climate of an organization. Too often these executives have an abstract conception of how work gets accomplished and order is maintained.[36] Their realistic or business orientation often precludes the sort of theoretical discussion that has been a vital part of this chapter. This is not to say that managers must become philosophers, but that they must appreciate the subtleties of the production process. What the Dreyfuses call "situated case studies" should become a central part

of instituting a MIS.[37] In other words, the ways in which management philosophy, the expectations of employees, and beliefs about
work, for example, affect the culture of an organization should be
recognized. Particularly important in this context, the general humanistic orientation adopted by a majority of social service employees should not be undermined by the expediency of managers.

2. The installation of a MIS should be inaugurated with an ethnographic study of an organization. Most often, however, actions
plans do not include this kind of contextual methodology.[38] Economic, logistical, and managerial considerations are usually high
on every planner's list of tasks that must be accomplished. Nonetheless, an ethnographic study will supply important insights with
respect to the criteria for identifying valid knowledge, the conditions
for successful communication, and contextually appropriate solutions to problems. Various methodological strategies may be used
to gain this sort of knowledge—questionnaires, observations, or
interviews. Particularly relevant is that a MIS project should begin
with research aimed at revealing the practical knowledge used by
employees to regulate their environment. Cultural sensitivity will
thus be promoted.

3. To secure employee support for building a MIS, planning
should start from the realm occupied by employees and move up-
ward. A holistic approach, as noted by Kanter, is required for
employees to feel comfortable with change. Technicians, in other
words, should not monopolize planning sessions. This method is
clearly consistent with the belief that culture is negotiated. Forced
compliance is always an option, but not one that is exceptionally
productive. Unless workers understand and see the worth of a project, they may withhold significant information. Therefore, accurate
definitions, concepts, and data categories may never be obtained.
Managers must remember that most persons do not respond fa-
vorably to blatant disregard for their culture. Employees have spent
years acquiring knowledge which they believe is valuable, and they
are typically reluctant to have this information publicly discredited.
This commitment to an organization's culture by its inhabitants
should not be disregarded.

4. The social context of communication must be grasped. Suggested by this statement is that communication does not occur
simply because information is conveyed. Utility, relevance, and the

modes of rationality that are operative, for instance, play a role in determining whether or not a transmission makes any sense. Communication, in other words, is based on shared meaning that is gradually established over time.[39] The idea at this juncture is that communication is a human enterprise and not necessarily related to maintaining structural continuity. Humans do not merely exchange information, but tacitly establish the conditions for receiving input. Unless a MIS takes into account these subtle factors, the accumulation and efficient transmission of information may have minimal impact on improving decision making. MIS designers should not forget that perception is pragmatic, and knowledge is not important simply because it is outlined by engineers.

5. The technical assimilation of information should be accompanied by social integration. Efficient systems design, in other words, should not be viewed as sufficient to insure the integration of knowledge. Of course, human networks should be utilized when planning the flow of information. But when new channels must be opened, the social conditions necessary for this to occur must be made available for the culture of an organization to expand. This requires that issues pertaining to organizational style be given consideration when planning a MIS. A loosely coupled organizational style, as described by Weick, may be appropriate for this undertaking.[40] By following this tactic, the natural alignments that are present can be enlarged without coercion. The integration of the various knowledge bases in an organization can thus take place with as little disruption as possible. For Weick claims that a loosely coupled organization is especially adept at "localized adaptation," since integration is not based on consensus but tolerance for differences.[41]

6. When a culture is negotiated, spontaneity is always possible. Indeed, creativity should not be viewed as anathema to order. Openness such as this must be retained subsequent to the implementation of a MIS. The reason for this is quite straightforward: A MIS will not be stifling. More to the point, the cognitive and other cultural demands imposed by a MIS will not necessarily become ominous. Criticism can be encouraged, so that an organization is not reified by a MIS. As might be suspected, retaining this sort of flexibility is vital to preparing an organization for change. Adaptability is fostered when a MIS is understood to be a framework for concep-

tualizing knowledge that is always subject to negotiation, similar to all other cultural artifacts. As a result, the installation of a MIS does not have to be traumatic. The culture of an organization, in other words, does not have to be misappropriated by a MIS.

## CONCLUSION

Obviously a MIS does not simply gather information. As is suggested by Peter Drucker, a MIS functions like a cognitive system.[42] The conditions are established, in other words, that enable knowledge to be identified, gathered, and disseminated in a particular way. Unfortunately, if managers and planners are not careful, these technical requirements may surreptitiously undermine the culture of an organization. The technical imagery that underpins MIS development may undermine the experiential knowledge that is used ordinarily for making decisions, solving problems, and averting interpersonal conflicts. In fact, these cultural considerations may be viewed as impediments to the systematic collection and transmission of information, for they represent soft information. When this is believed to be the case, an MIS often appears to be the only solution to the disorganization that often plagues service agencies. As a result, a technological fix is invoked to cure what may stem from more deep seated social problems.

The successful operation of an organization should not rely on this kind of technological ideology. Instead, management difficulties should be envisioned as tied ultimately to the culture of an organization. Proposing remedies that ignore this realm will likely prove to be fruitless. There is no shortcut to cultivating sound management practices. While working through the culture of an organization, reasonable goals, effective communication channels, sensible reporting requirements, and an orderly knowledge utilization plan can be established. However, these are qualitative and not quantitative activities. Most important about this chapter is that MIS development is assumed to be sustained by a qualitative dimension.[43] If this claim is ignored, a MIS will probably become obtrusive and thus disruptive. Information gathering will become nothing but a *tour de force*, an undertaking that will appropriate whatever data happens to be compatible with the system. Other, and possibly more pertinent, forms of knowledge may not receive any attention.

Unless planners are careful, a MIS may promote an artificial environment within an organization. Therefore, the qualitative side of MIS development should never be obscured. The everyday knowledge that guides the acquisition of data, communication, and the utilization of input must not be destroyed by systems design. MIS design should not be confused with social planning; establishing a MIS is a social project. Hence systems design engineers should not forget the social background of every MIS.

## NOTES

1. Karger, "The De-skilling of Social Workers: An Examination of the Industrial Mode of Production and the Delivery of Social Services," pp. 115-129.

2. Don Q. Matthews, *The Design of the Management Information System* (New York: Petrocelli/Charter, 1976), pp. 3-13.

3. Karen A. Callaghan and John W. Murphy, "Changes in Technological Social Control: Theory and Implications for the Workplace," in *The Underside of High-Tech*, ed. John W. Murphy, Algis Mickunas, and Joseph J. Pilotta (Westport, CT: Greenwood, 1986), pp. 15-28.

4. Bengt Abrahamsson, *Bureaucracy or Participation* (Beverly Hills: Sage, 1977), pp. 185-198.

5. Joseph Orlicky, *The Successful Computer System* (New York: McGraw-Hill, 1969), pp. 9-33.

6. James V. Milano, "Modular Method of Structuring MIS," in *MIS: Management Dimensions*, ed. Raymond J. Coleman and M.J. Riley (San Francisco: Holden-Day, 1973), p. 242.

7. Rosabeth Moss Kanter, *The Change Masters* (New York: Simon and Schuster, 1984), p. 29.

8. Ibid., p. 243.

9. Talcott Parsons, *Societies: Evolutionary and Comparative Perspectives* (Englewood Cliffs, NJ: Prentice-Hall, 1966), pp. 21-24.

10. David Dery, *Computers in Welfare* (Beverly Hills: Sage, 1981), p. 211.

11. Pamela McCorduck, *Machines Who Think* (San Francisco: W.H. Freeman, 1979), pp. 42-47.

12. Lyotard, *The Postmodern Condition*, pp. 11.

13. Harlan D. Mills, Richard C. Linger, and Alan R. Hevner, *Information Systems Analysis and Design* (New York: Academic Press, 1986), pp. 218-236.

14. Lee Thayer, "Communication Systems," in *The Relevance of System Theory*, ed. Ervin Laszlo (New York: George Braziller, 1972), p. 95-121.

15. Ibid, p. 96.

16. Mills, Linger, and Hevner, *Information Systems Analysis and Design*, pp. 316-339.

17. Denis Connor, *Information System Specification and Design Road Map* (Englewood Cliffs, NJ: Prentice-Hall, 1985), pp. 77-122.

18. Ibid., pp. 38-93.

19. Dery, *Computers in Welfare*, pp. 200-212.

20. Michael Shallis, *The Silicon Idol* (Oxford: Oxford University Press, 1984).

21. Pat-Anthony Federico, *Management Information Systems and Organizational Behavior* (New York: Praeger, 1985), pp. 138-150.

22. Lyotard, *The Postmodern Condition*, pp. 48ff.

23. Dery, *Computers in Welfare*, p. 233.

24. Deborah Namm, "The Case of the Changing Technology: Impact of Micro Computer Technology in a Fortune 500 Company," in *Technology and Human Productivity*, ed. John W. Murphy and John T. Pardeck (Westport, CT: Greenwood, 1986), pp. 95-101.

25. Dreyfus and Dreyfus, *Mind over Machine*, pp. 158-192.

26. Charles Perrow, *Complex Organizations* (New York: Random House, 1986), pp. 79-118.

27. Dreyfus and Dreyfus, *Mind over Machine*, pp. 163-167.

28. Linda Argote and Paul S. Goodman, "The Organizational Implications of Robotics," in *Managing Technological Innovation*, ed. Donald D. Davis and Associates (San Francisco: Jossey-Bass, 1986): pp. 127-153.

29. Karl Weick, "Educational Organizations as Loosely Coupled Systems," *Administrative Science Quarterly* 21(1) (1976): pp. 1-19.

30. Kanter, *The Change Masters*, pp. 143-155.

31. Karl Weick, *The Social Psychology of Organizing* (Reading, MA: Addison-Wesley, 1979), p. 164.

32. Lyotard, *The Postmodern Condition*, p. 10.

33. Weick, *The Social Psychology of Organizing*, pp. 140-154.

34. Paul Blumberg, "Alienation and Participation," in *Self-Management*, ed. Jaroslav Vanek (Middlesex, England: Penguin Books, 1975), pp. 324-338.

35. Egon Bittner, "The Concept of Organization," in *Ethnomethodology*, ed. Roy Turner (Baltimore: Penguin, 1974), p. 76.

36. Federico, *Management Information Systems*, pp. 25-30.

37. Dreyfus and Dreyfus, *Mind over Machine*, pp. 167-170.

38. Karl E. Weick, "Educational Organizations as Loosely Coupled Systems," in *Complex Organizations: Critical Perspectives*, ed. Mary Zey-

Ferrell and Michael Aiken (Glenview, IL: Scott, Foresman, and Company, 1981), p. 225.

39. Jürgen Habermas, *Legitimation Crisis* (Boston: Beacon Press, 1975), p. 10.

40. Weick, "Educational Organizations as Loosely Coupled Systems," p. 219.

41. Ibid., p. 222.

42. Joseph J. Pilotta and John Murphy, "Program Evaluation as a Facilitator of Rational Decision Making," *The Journal of Applied Social Sciences* 6(1) (1981-82): pp. 11-26.

43. John W. Murphy and John T. Pardeck, "Important Nontechnical Considerations in the Development of an MIS System," pp. 129-136.

# 5

## Technical Adjuncts to Intervention

The role of the computer in clinical activities has expanded rapidly during the 1980s. Presently, psychologists, psychiatrists, and small numbers of clinical social workers are using the new computer technologies in treatment. Often, it is argued, computers can perform many therapeutic tasks more cheaply, efficiently, and reliably than humans, because computer programs are standardized and thus unaffected by personal biases.[1]

The computer can be a useful, therapeutic tool capable of interacting with clients, identifying symptoms, and rendering clinical assessments. In fact, some practitioners claim that the computer-assisted diagnoses are more valid than those produced by trained therapists.[2] Thus the claim is made that computers should be implemented in a wide range of therapies.

However, the use of computers in therapy has not gone unchallenged; numerous questions have been raised about the dehumanizing effects this technology may have on the therapeutic process.[3] But, the criticisms that have been lodged against the computer have been mostly related to the logistical problems associated with their implementation.[4] The overall appropriateness of computers in clinical practice has not been seriously doubted; rather, suggestions have been made mostly about improving the human-technological

interface. These proposals relate to changes in preparing practitioners for practice, the nature of their work, and the organizational
structure of human services agencies.

During the 1950s, claims were made that statistical predictions
are more accurate than decisions based on clinical intuition. This
charge inaugurated a trend that continues today. That is, if clinicians
are to ever achieve a scientific status, their judgements must begin
to reflect rigorous standards. So-called scientific data, in other
words, must be available to justify diagnoses and other aspects of
intervention.

As is argued throughout this book, computers are thought to be
capable of bringing this dream to fruition. After all, what is more
in tune with the precepts of science than a computer? For clearly,
computerization is able to facilitate the objectification of information. Computers can thus help clinicians gain the legitimacy they
so desperately desire, charge the proponents of computerization.

This obsession with becoming scientific, however, has played a
large part in limiting the critiques of computerization. Once the
outlook engendered through science is accepted, only certain questions can be raised. Mostly these relate to the technical aspects of
research and intervention. Challenging the entire scientific enterprise is considered to be illegitimate. As a result, the criticisms
clinicians have expressed about the use of computer technology
have not been trenchant. Technical remedies for logistical problems
have been the primary focus of attention.

One must keep the above points in mind when attempting to
understand the significance of computers in conducting therapy.
The following discussion will focus on computer-based adjuncts to
therapy, including how this technology is currently being used in
the diagnoses of clinical problems.

## COMPUTERIZED TESTING AND INVENTORIES

Slack, Hicks, Reed, and VanCura did much of the early development of computer-based psychological testing and assessment.[5]
Their key contribution is a computer-based medical interview that
is extremely crude by today's standards. The program used a fairly
refined branching logic, which provided patients with cues to assist
them throughout the interview. The initial evaluations of the pro-

gram were positive, and subsequently the way was paved for more sophisticated developments in computer-assisted assessment and testing.

In the two and a half decades following the initial work by Slack and his colleagues, computer-based assessment has burgeoned. For example, instruments such as the Minnesota Multiphasic Personality Inventory (MMPI) have been computerized. In this case, proponents contend that the primary benefit of the computer is the ability to combine the strengths of standard paper-and-pencil clinical instruments with the intelligence and flexibility of a clinician. Since the program performs exactly as instructed, complete reliability in the interviewing process is always present. Indeed, the computer never forgets a question and always follows the same format. In fact, Carr, Ghost, and Ancill found that computerized psychiatric histories obtained five and a half items per client that were not recorded by a practitioner, including such clinically significant information as having attempted suicide (17 percent) and having a criminal record (26 percent).[6] Standardized questionnaires provide the same benefits, but the computer can provide flexibility by differentially responding to an individual client's input. These new developments in computer-assisted assessment, with supporting research findings, clearly suggest that a number of exciting developments have occurred with regard to making computerized diagnoses.

Who could deny that computer-assisted assessment enhances data integrity? After all, a computer can prevent the proliferation of incomplete questionnaires by repeating or rephrasing a question until a client responds. Furthermore, a computer can be programmed to accept only valid responses for a particular questionnaire item, thus preventing incorrect input. Validity checks can also be performed, and key questions may be asked again if inconsistent or unclear responses are obtained. Lastly, by generating results directly from a computer-compatible format, computerized clinical test administration facilitates the scoring of long and complicated instruments. No recording or transcription of responses by the therapist is required, thereby minimizing one potential source of errors.

Two dimensions according to which computer-based assessment can be classified are (1) the content of the assessment instrument and (2) the degree to which the program is interactive with the user.[7] Even though there have been a number of positive developments in the area of computerized assessment, including the incorporation of flexible branching, such systems require more research and must be understood in terms of how they have the potential to dehumanize a client.

The easiest way to create a computerized clinical instrument is simply to copy an existing standard clinical inventory. A critical methodological concern in this case is to insure that the computer inventory has the same psychometric properties as the paper-and-pencil questionnaire on which it is based. An excellent example of this is the computerized MMPI test. Between the computer-assisted MMPI and the paper-and-pencil questionnaire on which it is based, high correlations and comparable mean scores have been noted. These findings are also true of such inventories as the Marital Adjustment Test, the Beck Depression Inventory, the Trait Anxiety Inventory, and the Wechsler Adult Intelligence Scale.[8]

The computer-based instruments that appear to have the most promise may well be those where the computer's flexibility in branching is used. A prime example of this kind of instrument is the interview schedule developed by Griest to assess the risk of suicide.[9] An illustration of the power of branching capabilities is provided when asking detailed questions about a previous suicide attempt if one has occurred, but skipping over these items if a client has never taken such an action. Griest's research team found in retrospective evaluation, where both the computer and clinician made predictions based on case histories, the computer was more accurate than the practitioner.

Wodarski has done an excellent job at enumerating the computerized assessment inventories that are available for use on a personal computer.[10] As the discussion above emphasizes, these inventories continue to be developed at a rapid rate. In fact, if the clinician does not have a personal computer available for scoring these instruments, the national computer system's professional services has the facilities necessary to score assessment inventories for clinicians in (1) normal personality, (2) abnormal personality, (3) aptitudes and career/vocation interests, and finally, (4) behavioral health and medicine.[11] Examples of the inventories that are available are as follows:

- Adjective Checklist
- Bender Visual Motor Gestalt Test
- California Psychological Inventory
- Career Assessment Inventory
- Clinical Analysis Questionnaire
- The Exner Report for the Rorschach Comprehensive System
- General Aptitude Test Battery
- Giannetti On-Line Psychosocial History
- Guilford-Zimmerman Temperament Survey
- Hogan Personality Inventory
- Millon Adolescent Personality Inventory—Clinical
- Millon Adolescent Personality Inventory—Guidance
- Millon Behavioral Health Inventory
- Minnesota Multiphasic Personality Inventory (MMPI) Basic Service
- MMPI—The Minnesota Report: Adult Clinical System
- MMPI—The Minnesota Report: Personnel Selection System
- Multidimensional Personality Questionnaire
- Myers-Briggs Type Indicator
- The Rorschach Comprehensive System
- Self-Description Inventory
- Sixteen Personality Factors Questionnaire
- Strong-Campbell Interest Inventory
- Temperament and Values Inventory
- Vocational Information Profile
- Word and Number Assessment Inventory

Before concluding this discussion on the developments in the area of computerized assessment, a number of important criticisms concerning this technology need to be presented.

Pardeck concludes that computerized assessment is sustained by the logic of positive science, and thus the type of data that is deemed valuable is severely truncated.[12] But as many clinicians realize, clinical assessment consists of judgments, rather than simply deductive arguments. While computers are not affected by everyday concerns, this sort of uninvolved decision making may be clinically disastrous.

Erdman and others have suggested that computerized interviewing is so radically different from traditional forms of interviewing, the long-term impact of computerized interviews are difficult to assess.[13] Another important concern with this new technology is that a vast amount of data can be gathered. The result may well be a glut of confusing information, which is likely to overwhelm most clinicians.[14] Decision making is thus not really enhanced. While this issue may be viewed as essentially a methodological problem, when a practitioner's judgments are impaired, ethical concerns are evident.

Additionally, Spitzer argues that the validity of computerized interviewing may be difficult to assess, since this new technology cannot be compared to the usual unstructured clinical interview.[15] For example, a number of papers have reported the problems inherent in placing clients in front of a computer terminal for any reason. Particularly noteworthy, clients often tend to become passive when they are confronted by a computer.[16] Also, during the computerized interview, the factors that supply the context for behavior are minimized. Yet many modern writers contend that a comprehensive assessment must include an examination of a client's total social environment. However, computers do not fare well in this sort of unstructured analysis.[17]

## EXPERT SYSTEMS AND INTERVENTION

Computer programs have been available for some time that can play checkers, although none of them at an advanced level. Due to recent developments, however, more sophisticated programs have been created to undertake a wide range of tasks.[18] As is discussed in chapter 2, the purpose of these systems is to replicate the decision making ability of experts, without the capriciousness that is sometimes exhibited by humans.

Clearly many routine decisions can be made by a computer, thus reducing the costs of operating an agency. Various technicians argue that once the protocol used for decision making are identified, these rules can be built into a software package. Once experts are probed to discover the criteria they use when making decisions, this information is adopted uncritically to guide further inquiries. And following the codification of this input, the decision-making ability of practitioners is thought to be reinforced.

How does the logic of an expert system unfold and how are decisions reached? With input and output strategically matched, a hyphothetical diagnosis, transformed into computerized clinical practice, can be rendered. For every symptom, a remedy is prescribed. A good example of this approach is offered by INTERN-IST–1, a program for making diagnoses in internal medicine.[19] Furthermore, the DSM-IIIR is based on a similar format. But in order to evaluate this form of clinical diagnosis, computerization must be understood to represent a self-contained system of concepts.[20] This is what Dennett means when he states that learning is unimportant in the operation of expert systems.[21]

If cognition is understood to operate like a machine, then programming a computer to reason is possible. Even though the relationship between the mind and knowledge can be conceived in a causal manner, this model is very restrictive. Clarity and procedural rigor are assumed to be sufficient for generating judgments that are socially meaningful. When the mind is assumed to be equivalent to a physical system, goodness of fit between its parts is most important. A smooth running machine must have components which tightly mesh together.[22]

Establishing an adequate knowledge base is critical to creating an expert system. But the structural primitives that constitute this body of information demand that clear boundaries be outlined with respect to knowledge commonly accepted, for example, about relationships, facts, priorities, and purposes.[23] And because the responses elicited by input are regulated by the stored knowledge presupposed by a program, the emotional or interpretive side of knowledge is disregarded. Nonetheless, these scripts are believed to contain all information necessary for a person to make sound judgements.[24]

Prototypical elements that are essential to identifying a specific phenomena are accepted as representing reality. As a result, these factors delimit the range of rational inquiry. When a piece of information fits into the analytical scheme programmed into the system, thinking appears to be exhibited by the computer. Winogard argues that an expert system functions according to a style of programming that isolates a "miniworld," which is a facsimile of every-day life.[25] Due to this tactic, an expert system appears to behave and reason like an expert. This is because the range of possible responses is so restricted.

But expert systems and human cognition do not operate in a similar manner. If this were the case, the mind could be structured according to functionalist principles.[26] Cognition could be neatly divided into a series of mental activities, with each one assigned a particular task to perform. As such, each component of the mind could be understood as activated by a single stimulus in the environment. Conceived in this manner, the mind would be a data processor that requires only clear information channels in order to process and regulate knowledge.

Dreyfus and Dreyfus conclude that such a model for the mind can easily be mistaken as a system which enhances decision making, for thinking is equated with a person's ability to analyze input effectively and efficiently.[27] And since an expert system can accommodate vast amounts of data, the power of the mind is believed to be increased.[28] This ability to process large amounts of data in a precise manner is thought to enhance rational action, because data the mind could not ordinarily handle can be introduced regularly into the decision making process.

The most obvious shortcoming for clinical practice is that expert systems are based on an incomplete knowledge base, since only so-called objective features can be introduced in the decision making process. But how can intuition be purged from decision making without destroying cognition? At most, the conclusion can be reached that an expert system does not make the world more rational, but only outlines the rules that are required for this technology to function.

What does this mean to agency personnel who wish to use expert systems in the treatment process? Simply put, decision making related to treatment will not necessarily be enhanced through reliance on these expert systems. For clinical decisions are always context-bound, and thus asocial deductions do not have much utility. Values, beliefs, and other similarly interpretive factors are crucial to clinical practice, but alien to an expert system. Although expert systems clearly make the acquisition and utilization of knowledge precise, this outcome may not necessarily be productive in clinical practice. After all, diagnoses are seldom unambiguous and easily justified.

## COMPUTERS AND THERAPEUTIC INTERVENTION

The most controversial issue associated with computer use in human services agencies pertains to therapeutic intervention. Weizenbaum designed the program ELIZA, later to be expanded by Colby into DOCTOR, to simulate Rogerian therapy. Although ELIZA is somewhat crude, this program serves as the prototype for most interactive programs.[29] The belief was that if a client could begin a relationship with a computer, a great forward leap could be made in terms of simulating a therapeutic encounter. But many problems intervened to stifle the realization of this prospect.

Programs such as ELIZA appear to be conducting therapy. Closer examination suggests, however, they do not. For example, ELIZA scans input for specific words (*yes* answers to a query) and has several canned responses for any unit of input. As should be expected, given the complexity of language, conversation between the client and ELIZA gradually becomes nonsensical. In the next chapter, the logic used in ELIZA, and the inability of this program to handle language in an adroit manner, will be examined in more detail.

The program invented by Colby also functions by identifying keys (words, characters, or phrases) in a subject's input, and subsequently generates a response matched to a key word or phrase, or places key words or phrases into a context designed to elicit further input (e.g. by asking the respondent, "Why do you feel *x*?"). The program is also able to keep track of input for later use, including new keys. Another function of the program is to respond differentially depending on whether a key appears in the beginning, middle, or end of the treatment session.

At the time of their initial report, Colby and his colleagues announced that clients found their program to be frustrating. Suggested by this finding, according to Colby, is that further research is needed to test a significantly larger dictionary of both input responses and keys, as well as to improve program flexibility. He also offered the fascinating observation that researchers should consider not only modeling programs on current psychotherapeutic intervention, but also explore other unique models of client-computer interaction. Although this sounds promising, Colby does not really explore any alternatives. In this regard, his commitment to the narrow range of options presupposed by computer logic becomes obvious.

## NOVEL INTERVENTIONS

Over the last two decades there has been a rapid increase of interest and effort in the development of innovative intervention programs. In the following discussion, these inventions are grouped according to their area of application.

### Anxiety Disorders

Lang was the first person to apply computer technology to the modification of phobias.[30] He created DAD (Device for Automated Desensitization), a program that involves several important functions: (1) instruction and muscle relaxation, (2) a previously collected hierarchy of fear-arousing stimuli, and (3) a series of behavioral interventions, including instructions for imagining fear-arousing stimuli, relaxing, and inquiring about the extent of a client's fear response. Physiological data are collected concurrently with the subject's interaction with the program. As therapy begins, the respondent controls the progression through the hierarchy by a switch located on a chair. Later developments of DAD include a more detailed strategy for inquiring about a respondent's visualization, as well as instructions for increasing visualization skills.

Lang has continued his work on DAD and has reported some success with this program.[31] He conducted a controlled study in which three groups were compared: a DAD treatment group, another group that received treatment from a therapist, and a control group. The findings suggested that subjects treated with DAD demonstrated comparable or superior outcomes to clients treated by a human therapist. The DAD group also maintained improvement as well or better than the other treatment group after eight months following the intervention. These results suggest that DAD may be used as part of an effective desensitization procedure.

A research group at the Institute of Psychiatry in London has also published research findings that conclude a computer can be used in the assessment and treatment of phobias.[32] The research group, consisting of Carr, Gosh, Margo, and Ancill, developed an automated treatment program that consists of five major components: phobia assessment, treatment planning, weekly assessment and review, outcome, and follow-up. The program offers great promise in the treatment of phobias such as agoraphobia and social phobia.

Research by Biglan, Villwock, and Wick also report positive results for treating test anxiety.[33] The treatment consists of audiotaped relaxation training and computer-assisted desensitization techniques. Suggested by the research is that the program reduced anxiety in subjects.

A program recently developed by Muehlenhard includes widely accepted principles of assertiveness training, including corrective feedback, rehearsal, modeling, and coaching.[34] The fully automated Muehlenhard program has been compared with two other treatment groups that received similar training through traditional methods. The results illustrate that those treated by Muehlenhard's program did as well as the clients who were treated in a traditional fashion.

### Affective Disorders

The program MORTON has been found to be effective in treating depression. MORTON is based on the cognitive-behavioral intervention principles proposed by Beck.[35] MORTON consists of six to eight treatment sessions, with each one lasting approximately fifty minutes. The initial session consists of attempts to establish rapport and other components critical to successful therapy. Once therapy begins, the Beck Depression Inventory (BDI) is administered after each session. Throughout treatment, MORTON provides a client with information essential to identifying cognitive distortions, along with suggestions about how to manage thought processes during future depressive episodes. MORTON has been compared to human therapeutic intervention for depression, and the results suggest this program is as effective as a human therapist.

Recent research by Lawrence described a more circumscribed,

but potentially valuable, program for treating depression.[36] The program is based on homework assignments that stress a cognitive-behavioral view of depression. Included are assessment and feedback materials, along with logs to record the mood and behavior of clients. These items are included to enhance self-monitoring and to provide clients with insight into their cognitive-behavioral patterns.

### Child/Adolescent Behavior Dysfunction

Behavioral approaches to treatment are easily adapted to computer-assisted therapy. The program BEHAVIOR MANAGER is an excellent example of such an adaption to the classroom setting.[37] The program utilizes information provided by the teacher about a child with behavioral problems, the teachers' preferences for changing behavior, and a plan of action for teacher intervention.

Computer games also have been used for treating children with some success.[38] Allen reports that computer games such as UL-TIMA, a game based on Dungeons and Dragons, can assist in the therapeutic process. He reports that many of a child's frustrations and problems are revealed as he or she plays the game. During this process, the impulsive child learns to plan ahead and be more cautious, while the timid child learns to take risks. As the child plays the game, the therapist can take a number of roles. The therapist can give advice, help a child apply the game's experiences to real-life problems, or provide support when the child becomes frustrated and point out the appropriate lesson to be learned from the experience. Allen concludes that children who complete his game therapy appear to have more self-confidence, a better sense of mastery, a greater willingness to accept responsibility for themselves, and fewer negative feelings about having been in therapy.

Adolescents can learn impulse control through a computer game developed by Clark and Schoech.[39] This program incorporates the principles of both play therapy and cognitive behavioral training. The program consists of a fantasy-adventure type game, which presents various scenarios that provide a child with the opportunity to make decisions. Children earn or lose points based on their problem-solving skills. The initial research findings suggest that the program may prove useful as a therapeutic tool; however, more evaluation must be done to determine its effectiveness.

## Problem Solving

Wagman and Kerber have developed a program called PLATO-DCS for aiding clients in clarifying and resolving difficulties in making choices.[40] This program is designed to help clients deal with a wide range of problems. The program guides clients through five steps: (1) formulating the problem, (2) helping the client make choices between conflicting solutions, (3) rephrasing the problem in a more positive way that permits positive outcomes, (4) generating solutions, and (5) ranking and evaluating the solutions.

Evaluation of PLATO-DCS by subjects suggests the program is helpful in teaching problem-solving skills.[41] Subjects also indicated a preference for PLATO-DCS over human counselors, while the majority of clients did not feel the program was impersonal. Also revealed by controlled studies is that the program does improve clients' problem-solving abilities.[42]

## Educational/Vocational Counseling

Sampson has found computers to be useful in counseling clients to make educational/vocational choices.[43] He has distinguished between information systems and guidance systems. Information systems aid clients in identifying the characteristics of desired jobs, and in obtaining information about careers. Guidance systems provide a broader range of functions, including helping a client to clarify job related values, along with planning and evaluating the success of vocational plans.

Intervention programs have also provided assistance in more specific areas, including clarifing values, acquiring study skills, and appraising health risks.[44] Other areas suggested for further development are assertiveness training, conflict resolution, parent training, and stress management.[45]

## Weight Management

Recently, Burnett, Taylor, and Agras have developed a program to treat obesity.[46] The program provides on-line behavioral treatment of obesity via a portable microcomputer. The program requires clients to self-monitor food consumption at meals and snacks, in addition to documenting exercise duration and exertion level. The program calculates the total caloric intake for each meal or snack, total calorie consumption on a given day, and the remaining calorie allotment for a twenty-four hour period.

Indications from a controlled study are that the program is more effective than paper-and-pencil methods for self-monitoring weight loss.[47] Furthermore, the computer-assisted groups were able to maintain continued weight loss over an extended time period.

### Sexual Dysfunction

Binik, Servan-Schreiber, and Hall have developed a computer program to treat sexual dysfunction.[48] Their program, called SEXPERT, demonstrates the feasibility of developing an intelligent dialogue based on examination and treatment by an expert system. SEXPERT works by introducing its limitations to the client, and then proceeds to gather background information, conduct an assessment, provide a diagnosis, present factors that may contribute to sexual dysfunction, and offer treatment for this problem. Recent research suggests that SEXPERT has great potential for treating sexual dysfunction. However, more empirical testing is needed.

### CONCLUSION

Clearly, significant advancements in the area of computerized therapy have occurred. As microcomputer technology advances, however, two important questions must be explored. What differentiates the treatment provided by a computer from that offered by a human therapist? What is it about treatment by a human therapist that is so important?[49]

With regard to the first question, human therapists have the capability to be much more flexible and responsive than a machine. As is argued throughout this book, this difference stems from the way in which issues must be conceived during intervention mediated by a computer.

The programs discussed in this chapter provide examples of this claim. Each one has met with some of success. But the question must be asked, have the problems they deal with been defined in such a way that successful treatment is likely? If a complex issue is differentiated far enough, merely one aspect of it may receive attention. As a result, the illusion can be created that substantial behavioral change has occurred, when, in fact, a readily identifiable variable has been temporarily manipulated. In the therapeutic applications just mentioned, the familial, economic, or other cultural or social conditions that are integral to each malady are ignored.

But this type of asocial research must not become normative, for variables that are easily isolated, altered, and measured tend to be the focus of this research. In this sense, statistical significance is substituted for social importance when research findings are discussed. What does this type of research prove? Anyone can establish certain conditions and then measure what those factors have been designed to illustrate. And if these definitions are narrow enough, monumental changes may seem to have taken place. In none of the research discussed is there any indication that understanding occurred, although moderately positive findings have been reported. Why changes were witnessed is purely speculative.

The second question pertains to the significance of the therapeutic relationship. This association encompasses the encounter between two human beings who form a genuine, authentic bond designed to produce change at the deepest levels of the human experience. The work of Freud provides a key example that the human encounter is the primary tool for therapeutic change.[50] In this case, change occurs through the process of transference. Anna Freud supported this principle in her work as well. She concluded, "With due respect for the necessary strictest handling and interpretation of the transference, I feel that we should leave room somewhere for the realization that the analyst and patient are also two real people of equal adult status, in a real personal relationship with each other."[51]

Other therapists such as Rogers, Truax, and Flanders all stress that empathy, warmth, and genuineness contribute significantly to a positive treatment outcome.[52] Mackey summarizes the importance of these factors

The most viable resource in clinical work is the self of the therapist—the self as represented in one's biopsychosocial history tempered by professional knowledge, values and skills...The reality that one human being has sought another for assistance suggests that the empathic presence of the latter has a special and potentially profound effect on the outcome of work between them.[53]

A computer cannot provide the many important ingredients critical to therapy that can be offered by human beings, including empathy, warmth, genuineness, authenticity, and the transference process that Freud and others saw as vital to a productive intervention. No matter how sophisticated the program, these factors have not been programmed into a computer. Unless there are radical changes in how therapy is viewed by mainstream therapists, the computer will continue to serve, at most, in a supportive role during the treatment process.

These critics are suggesting that key to successful therapy are elements positive scientists believe are unrelated to factual and reliable knowledge. They are making a point that should not be missed. That is, therapy is different from science and will probably never become scientific in the positivistic sense. The kind of interpersonal intimacy that is integral to therapy is denied legitimacy by positivists.

## NOTES

1. John H. Griest, et al., " A Computer Interview for Suicide Risk Prediction, " *American Journal of Psychiatry* 130 (4) (1973): pp. 1327-1332.

2. Morton Wagman, "PLATO DCS: An Interactive Computer System for Personal Counseling," *Journal of Counseling Psychology* 26 (1) (1980): pp. 16-30.

3. Murphy and Pardeck, "Technologically-Mediated Therapy: A Critique," pp. 605-612.

4. Marc D. Schwartz, "People in the Organization: The Effects of Computer-Mediated Work on Individuals and Organizations," in *Using Computers in Clinical Practice*, ed. Marc D. Schwartz (New York: The Haworth Press, 1984), pp. 55-59.

5. W. V. Slack, G. P. Hicks, C. Z. Reed, and L. J. VanCura, "A Computer-based Medical History System," *New England Journal of Medicine*, 274 (4) (1966): pp. 194-198.

6. A. C. Carr, A. Ghosh, R. R. Ancill, "Can A Computer Take a Psychiatric History?" *Psychological Medicine* 13 (1) (1983): pp. 151-158.

7. Sharon W. Foster and Harold P. Erdman, "Computer-Assisted Psychological Assessment and Intervention," in *Computers in Human Services: An Overview for Clinical and Welfare Services*, ed. John T. Pardeck and John W. Murphy (London: Harwood Academic Publishers, 1990), pp. 35-54.

8. Ibid., p. 38

9. Griest, "A Computer Interview for Suicide Risk Prediction," pp. 1327-1332.

10. Wodarski, "Development of Management Information Systems for Human Services: A Practical Guide," pp. 37-49.

11. Ibid., pp. 41-42.

12. John T. Pardeck, "Microcomputer Technology in Clinical Practice: An Analysis of Ethical Issues," *Journal of Independent Social Work* 2 (1) (1987): pp. 76-81.

13. Harold P. Erdman, et al., "The Computer Psychiatrist: How Far Have We Come? Where Are We Heading? How Far Can We Go?" *Behavioral Research Methods and Instrumentation* 13 (4) (1981): pp. 393-398.

14. John T. Pardeck, "Microcomputer Technology in Clinical Practice: An Analysis of Ethical Issues," *Philosophy and Social Action* 15(1–2) (1989): pp. 43-50.

15. Robert L. Spitzer, "Psychiatric Diagnosis: Are Clinicians Still Necessary," *Comprehensive Psychiatry* 24(4) (1983): pp. 401-410.

16. Mike Fitter, "The Development of Information Technology in Health Care," in *Information Technology and People*, ed. Frank Blackles and David Oborne (Cambridge: MIT Press, 1987), pp. 105-127.

17. Harvey A. Skinner and Barbara A. Allen, "Does the Computer Make A Difference? Computerized Versus Face-to-Face Versus Self-Report Assessment of Alcohol, Drug, and Tobacco Use," *Journal of Consulting and Clinical Psychology* 52(2) (1983): pp. 267-275; Weizenbaum, "ELIZA—Computer Program for the Study of Natural Language Communication Between Man and Machine," *Communications Association For Computer Machinery* 9 (1) (1966): pp. 36-45.

18. John W. Murphy and John T. Pardeck, "Expert Systems as an Adjunct to Clinical Practice: A Critique," in *Computer In Human Services: An Overview for Clinical and Welfare Services*, ed. John T. Pardeck and John W. Murphy (London: Harwood Academic Publishers, 1990), pp. 75-86.

19. Ibid., pp. 75-76.

20. Dreyfus, *What Computers Can't Do*, pp. 42-63.

21. Daniel Dennett, "Cognitive Wheels: The Frame Problem of AI," in *Minds, Machines, and Evolution*, ed. Christopher Hookway (Cambridge: Cambridge University Press, 1984), pp. 129-151

22. Murphy and Pardeck, "Expert Systems as an Adjunct to Clinical Practice: A Critique," p. 84.

23. Marvin Minsky and Seymour Papert, "Artificial Intelligence." London Lectures, Oregon State of Higher Education, Eugene, Oregon, 1973.

24. Roger Schank and Robert Abelson, *Scripts, Plans, Goals, and Understanding* (Hillsdale, NJ: Lawrence Eilbraum Associates, 1977), pp. 36-68.

25. Terry Winograd, *Understanding Natural Language* (New York: Academic Press, 1972), pp. 23-38.

26. John W. Murphy and John T. Pardeck, "The Computer Microworld, Knowledge and Social Planning," *Computers and Human Services* 3(1/2) (1988): pp. 127-142.

27. Dreyfus and Dreyfus, *Mind Over Machine*, pp. 103-106.

28. Ibid., pp. 158-192.

29. Pardeck, "Microcomputer Technology in Clinical Practice: An Analysis of Ethical Issues," pp. 60-64.

30. Peter J. Lang, "The On-Line Computer in Behavior Therapy Research," *American Psychologist*, 24(3) (1969): pp. 236-239.

31. Peter. J. Lang, "Behavioral Treatment and Biobehavioral Assessment: Computer Applications," in *Technology in Mental Health Care Delivery Systems*, pp. 129-138.

32. A. C. Carr, R. J. Ancill, A. Ghosh, and A. Margo, "Direct Assessment of Depression by Microcomputer," *Acta Psychiatric Scandinavia* 64 (4) (1981): pp. 415-422.

33. Anthony Biglan, Carolyn Villwock, and Steve Wick, "The Feasibility of a Computer Controlled Program for the Treatment of Test Anxiety," *Journal of Behavior Therapy and Experimental Psychiatry*, 10(1) (1979): pp. 47-49.

34. Charlene, L. Muehlenhard, "Comparison of Fully and Semiautomated Assertion Training." Ph.D. diss. University of Wisconsin, Madison, 1981.

35. Aaron T. Beck, John A. Rush, Brian F. Shaw, and Gary Emergy, *Cognitive Therapy of Depression* (New York: Guilford, 1979), pp. 142-166.

36. G. H. Lawrence, "Using Computers for the Treatment of Psychological Problems," *Computers in Human Behavior* 2(1) (1981): pp. 43-62.

37. Jerry R. Tomlinson, Nancy E. Acher, and J. Patrick Mathien, *The Behavior Manager* (Minneapolis: ATM, 1984).

38. David H. Allen, "The Use of Computer Fantasy Games in Child Therapy," in *Using Computers in Clinical Practice*, ed. Marc D. Schwartz (New York: The Haworth Press, 1984), pp. 330-333.

39. B. Clark and D. Schoech, "A Computer Assisted Therapeutic Game

for Adolescents: Initial Development and Comments," *Computers in Psychiatry/Psychology*, 5(1) (1983): pp. 7-20.

40. Morton Wagman and Kenneth Kerber, "PLATO-DCS: An Interactive Computer System for Personal Counseling: Further Development and Evaluation," *Journal of Counseling Psychology* 27(1) (1980): pp. 31-39.

41. Ibid., p. 38

42. Ibid., p. 38

43. James P. Sampson, "An Integrated Approach to Computer Applications in Counseling Psychology," *Counseling Psychologist*, 11(4) (1983): pp. 65-74.

44. Ibid., p. 70.

45. Ibid., p. 70.

46. Kent F. Burnett, C. Barr Taylor, and W. Stewart Agras, "Ambulatory Computer-Assisted Therapy for Obesity: A New Frontier for Behavior Therapy," *Journal of Consulting and Clinical Psychology* 53(5) (1985): pp. 698-703.

47. Ibid., p. 702.

48. Forster and Erdman, "Computer-Assisted Psychological Assessment and Intervention," pp. 45-46.

49. John T. Pardeck, "Microcomputer Technology in Clinical Practice: An Overview of Ethical Concerns," in *Computers in Human Services: An Overview for Clinical and Welfare Services*, ed. John T. Pardeck and John W. Murphy (London: Harwood Academic Publishers, 1990), pp. 55-65.

50. Ibid., p. 63.

51. Anna Freud, "The Widening Scope of Indicators for Psychoanalysis," *Journal of the American Psychoanalytic Association* 2 (1954): p. 609.

52. Pardeck, "Microcomputer Technology in Clinical Practice: An Overview of Ethical Concerns," p. 63.

53. Rich A. Mackey, *Ego Psychology and Clinical Practice* (New York: Gardner Press, 1954), p. 74.

# 6

---

# Computer-Mediated Therapy

## INTRODUCTION

At this time, computers are more than simply adjuncts to therapy. A variety of interactive programs have been invented that actually engage clients in dialogue. In a manner of speaking, computers have become surrogate therapists. Programs such as DOCTOR and ELIZA, for example, are able to respond to questions that are posed by clients, and thereby enter into a discussion with these persons. In fact, some research exists which suggests that clients do not mind interacting with a machine, and feel more comfortable divulging sensitive information to a computer than to a live therapist.[1] Clients seem to like the nonjudgmental approach taken by a computer to analyzing their problems.

What these persons appear to be describing is a successful catharsis. Because a computer is believed to be an inanimate object, clients express emotions that they would not otherwise vent. Talcott Parsons described this sort of anonymity when he discussed the "sick role."[2] In short, doctors are supposed to maintain a significant amount of social distance between themselves and their clients, thus facilitating an accurate exchange of information that would be awkward under normal conditions. Enhanced by computerization, in other words, is the professionalism that encourages intimacy between a practitioner and client. Yet when this is accomplished by a computer, is the therapeutic relationship really improved?

Intimacy is not supposed to be an end in itself. This kind of association is supposed to culminate in increased insight, and thus more accurate diagnoses. Most important at this juncture is that making an accurate diagnoses requires knowledge about a host of social conditions. In this regard, Thomas Szasz declares that "psychiatry is a moral and social enterprise," and "classification is a social act."[3] Yet can accurate information be forthcoming from computerized discourse, simply because interaction is deanimated? The therapeutic relationship, instead, must provide clients with much more than an opportunity for a catharsis. Stated simply, information must be exchanged; a common knowledge base must be accumulated for making sound clinical judgments.

Yet what kind of knowledge base can be the result of computerized discourse? This question is at the heart of the controversy surrounding the use of computers as therapists. Although a mechanical interface can be established between clients and computers, does such a relationship allow for the accumulation of insightful information? In this regard, serious questions have been raised pertaining to the quality of understanding and communication that is possible during computerized therapy. In fact, nowhere else does the issue of dehumanization become more visible than in discussions about computer-mediated therapy. Considering recent shifts in epistemology related to the contextual character of illness, many critics doubt whether therapy can be undertaken via a computer. Questions abound regarding the ability of computerized interaction to generate a valid knowledge base for making diagnoses. In short, doubts persist related to the social sensitivity of computer-mediated interaction.

Information must be communicated between a client and therapist in order for clinical judgments to be accurate. The fact that the word *communication* is derived from *communitas*, or "to share," is significant. Sharing knowledge allows for the establishment of a knowledge base that has relevance for both client and therapist. Hence a common frame of reference must be engendered between these persons; mutual understanding between them must be achieved. But is increased interpersonal contact sufficient to guarantee this outcome? As will be discussed later in this chapter, presupposed by computer-mediated therapy is a rendition of communication, and thus understanding, that may undermine the therapeutic relationship in the long run.

## COMPUTERS AS THERAPISTS

Language use and communication are usually identified as the traits that differentiate human beings from animals. It should be no surprise, therefore, that the development of computers able to interact with humans would be given high praise. For presupposed by interaction is the ability to interpret information intelligently and respond appropriately to certain cues. Hence, interactive programs are thought to represent state-of-the-art inventions, due to their apparent ability to appear interpersonally competent. No wonder practitioners were initially impressed by programs such as ELIZA, DOCTOR, and PLATO-DCS. After all, these devices appeared to be capable of replacing therapists. ELIZA, for example, appeared to engage clients in dialogue, and as a result obtain information from them that was garnered formerly by an interviewer.[4]

Work on these kinds of interactive software packages was inaugurated during the 1950s.[5] Key to their development were the advancements made in machine translations, game playing, and pattern recognition. The success that was witnessed in designing programs that could play games such as chess, for example, led engineers to believe that the development of machines that could converse with humans would not be far away. The problem facing interactive programs, however, was that a computer had to be able to recognize natural language acts, translate this input into programming instructions, and respond in a manner that makes sense within a particular social context.

In fact, a string of interactive programs—Oracle, SAD SAM, SIR, CONVERSATION MACHINE—eventually appeared. For example, CONVERSATION MACHINE chatted about the weather, while SAD SAM could answer questions about kinship relations. Yet these early developments were not very sophisticated, for the output produced hardly resembled the product of a conversation. For when persons who are linguistically competent engage in a conversation, they not only receive information but respond in a manner that indicates interest and perpetuates interaction. None of these original programs behaved as an interlocutor, but rather they performed merely as information processors. A reply simply followed a stimulus in a mechanistic manner.

Central to nonutilitarian interaction, on the other hand, is engagement, whereby persons are drawn together. A type of bonding occurs in a real conversation, when individuals begin to recognize that their lives overlap and they share experiences. Martin Buber described this as an "I-thou," as opposed to an "I-it," relationship. The thrust of a real conversation is to invite persons to reveal information about themselves, so that their knowledge of one another can be increased. According to Habermas, true dialogue involves the "cooperative search for truth."[6] As a result, greater intimacy is achieved. No pretense was made that this kind of social bond could be developed through the use of these programs.

By the mid-1960s, however, much more elaborate programs had been produced. Actually, ELIZA was created because of Weizenbaum's interest in natural language.[7] Due to the discovery of new techniques, a few simple linguistic transformations could now be made by computers. In other words, the illusion of engagement could be perpetrated. Colby, a psychiatrist, adapted ELIZA to a clinical setting, and thus DOCTOR appeared on the scene.[8] Improvements made in the ability of computers to handle natural language led many persons to believe that ELIZA and DOCTOR were capable of deep semantic analysis. Weizenbaum became concerned, however, that persons began to think that ELIZA had somehow demonstrated a "general solution to the problem of computer understanding of natural language."[9] Additionally, Weizenbaum worried that persons could be all too easily lured into talking about very sensitive topics with ELIZA. Hence the therapeutic implications of these two programs were readily apparent to both Colby and Weizenbaum.

Both ELIZA and DOCTOR responded with natural linguistic sentences to linguistic input. Additionally, statements made by clients could be transformed into questions, thereby giving the impression that these programs were interested in pursuing a conversation. If a client would say something that ELIZA or DOCTOR could not recognize, a response that is neutral but elicits further information would be forthcoming. In this sense, the illusion could be maintained that these programs were actively involved with clients or anyone else who came into contact with them. As a result, persons were often fooled by these devices and believed they were interacting with other humans. ELIZA and DOCTOR, in other words, passed the Turing test regularly with flying colors.

The dialogue that is generated by these programs is modeled after nondirective, Rogerian therapy, so the chances would be enhanced that ELIZA and DOCTOR would seem alive.[10] Weizenbaum believed that persons constantly strive to explain events, especially in novel or unknown situations. Although ELIZA's responses may not be as direct as might be expected in a normal conversation, in a therapeutic setting they appear to be satisfactory. In fact, an oblique response is often interpreted as an attempt to gain additional information.

A typical encounter with ELIZA proceeds in the following way.

Client (Female): Men are all alike.

ELIZA: In what way?

Client: They are always bugging us about something or other.

ELIZA: Can you think of an example?

Client: Well, my boyfriend made me come here.

ELIZA: Your boyfriend made you come here, that is interesting.

Client: He says I am depressed much of the time.

ELIZA: I am sorry to hear you are depressed.

ELIZA's reactions are preprogrammed. For example, when the word *alike* is discovered in a sentence, the program is designed to answer "In what way?" When the word *always* is used, ELIZA asks for a specific example. Additionally, ELIZA can appear to be sympathetic, because several key words can be reflexively transformed. Hence, *you* becomes *I*, *your* becomes *my*, and so forth.[11] "Tell me more about it" is the phrase ELIZA uses when no key words are recognized. In short, ELIZA appears to be conversant, particularly within the confines of a therapeutic setting where ambiguity, at least initially, will be tolerated by clients.

Like the early pattern recognition programs, ELIZA is designed to respond to carefully coded input. However, a process of matching and classification is utilized that cannot deal with very complex patterns. For example, the following exchange between a client and ELIZA becomes nonsensical, due to the difficult nature of the English language:

Client: Well, I can't explain.

ELIZA: How do you know you cannot explain?

Client: How does anyone know anything?

ELIZA: Why do you ask?

Client: Because I don't know.

ELIZA: Is that the real reason?

Client: You're the analyst, you tell me.

ELIZA: What makes you think I am the analyst, you tell you?[12]

Obviously, the subtleties of a conversation cannot be handled by ELIZA. A rhetorical question posed by the client (How does anyone know anything?) prompts an inappropriate question, because ELIZA is ignorant of the social context. Similar to all programs that make mechanistic translations, the intricacies of discourse are often missed. All that is possible is what some writers refer to as a "template," or standardized, response to situations that are presumed to be typical. As critics of ELIZA noted, the "illusion of deep semantic analysis" was simply created.[13]

Several key problems are associated with these word-for-word translations.[14] First, the context of communication is not taken into account. Second, ambiguous utterances can easily be addressed insensitively, because the social cues that are usually assessed in these cases are not available. Finally, the unstated purpose of a speech act can easily be misconstrued, as a result of literal interpretations. Would a competent speaker say "Why do you ask?" when someone asks "How does anyone know anything?" Of course not. In this instance the aim is not to gain information, but to establish a context for further interaction. An opening is offered for more analysis. Yet the social presuppositions of speech have not been built into ELIZA or DOCTOR.

More elaborate programs such as SHRDLU, created by Terry Winograd, have been designed to overcome this problem.[15] Instead of pattern recognition, SHRDLU operates on the basis of a microworld. In other words, a knowledge base of common sense information sustains this program. Through the use of basic programming methods, such as procedures, iteration, and recursion, SHRDLU can think on its feet, so to speak. Given certain input, a variety of conclusions can be deduced that were not originally a part of the program. Thus SHRDLU appears to be capable of reasoning, and thereby responding to requests in a flexible and socially sensitive manner. As a therapist, SHRDLU might fare much better than ELIZA and DOCTOR.

However, the development of SHRDLU brought to a head a problem that still plagues the field of artificial intelligence. Stated simply, the knowledge persons use to regulate their daily lives could not be introduced efficiently or effectively into this program. The problem is that this knowledge base is not only extremely large and varied, but is always changing as a result of different interpretations of reality. Because persons influence reality through their use of language, neither universal assumptions nor standardized rules for reasoning capture adequately how cognition operates. As a result, only the simplest realms can be computerized. For example, Winograd's seminal work was conducted on a block world, which consisted of building blocks of various sizes placed on a table. He admits that programs like SHRDLU are only able to deal with "tightly specified areas of meaning in an artificially formal conversation."[16] Clearly, this frame of reference is not as intricate as the world inhabited by clients. Manipulating blocks, for example, is much less difficult than attempting to understand clients and anticipate how they will behave in various situations. A client's world is not this obtrusive.

In general, the key shortcoming of computerized discourse is that it is organized in terms of "technical competence."[17] Interaction is envisioned to be a technical exercise, rather than a hermeneutical one. SHRDLU, for example, operates on the basis of "relations [that] are fixed and limited in an obvious way."[18] Mastery of a few basic technical operations is thought to lead to understanding. Doubtless, this is a mistake. As will be shown later on in this chapter, inaugurating and maintaining discourse is much more intricate than is assumed by ELIZA, DOCTOR, or SHRDLU.

## TECHNICAL DIALOGUE

At this juncture Georg Simmel's question, How is society possible? is certainly germane. The thrust of this query relates to the methods adopted to insure order. A therapeutic relationship, more-over, represents an exercise in the maintenance of order. After all, two or more persons must somehow coordinate their actions, so that they are able to exhibit mutual concern and understanding. Through some means individuals with disparate backgrounds, in-terests, and outlooks must begin to relate to one another. Surely the issue of order is at the heart of this process. Can therapy be thought to proceed without in-depth communication occurring be-tween a client and therapist?

Two models of order have been traditionally proposed.[19] The first is called ontological realism. In this case, reality is thought to be the basis of order. Because all normal minds are assumed to perceive reality in a similar manner, order is thought to prevail. This objective reality has been conceptualized in various ways. At one time or another during the growth of AI, formal logic, models of rational behavior, and universal programming protocol have been proposed to insure order. In each instance, order is preserved by an autonomous point of reference.

Ontological nominalism is a very different approach to viewing order. Instead of existing absolutely, order is thought to emerge from discursive practices. Order, in other words, does not constrain language use, but is based on speech acts. Through the give and take indigenous to interaction, order is negotiated.

Clearly, these two views have very different implications relative to conceiving the therapeutic relationship. Ignored by realism is that reality is a linguistic construct. Therefore, the definitions clients hold about their lives and environment are treated as unimportant for securing order. The argument at this juncture is that this sort of reductionism will eventually prove to be disastrous. Because an ultimate reality is invoked to coordinate interaction, the existence of clients may become dominated by an anomalous force. In this regard, Jacques Derrida writes that patients may be "crushed be-neath psychiatry."[20] More concretely, an abstract mode of under-standing may be introduced to unite a client and therapist. Therefore, the therapeutic relationship will be thoroughly distorted.

It should be stated at this point that computer-mediated therapy is not dehumanizing simply because machines are involved. Instead, and much more important, an inappropriate image of dialogue is advanced. A technical rendition of dialogue is presumed to be acceptable, and thus a client's wishes are treated as ancillary to the formation of a therapeutic relationship. In short, ontological realism goes unquestioned.

With regard to ELIZA and DOCTOR, dialogue is based on pattern recognition. Specific input, in short, is matched automatically with particular output. According to Wagman's description of PLATO-DCS, interaction proceeds according to "highly structured" protocols that are compatible with the if/then logic essential to computerization.[21] Additionally, particular beliefs about clients underpin these response patterns. Realism is in effect in each program because input and output are aligned by what is called a canonical language. This is a so-called higher-order language, one that is assumed to have unquestioned validity, that is used to unite thoughts with words and the acts involved in discourse. Hence, the illusion of communication is created because information appears to be transferred.

Yet is understanding a part of this process? John Searle maintains that this is not the case in his discussion of machine translations.[22] If persons are trained in English to recognize Chinese characters and respond appropriately when specific ones are presented, can it be said these individuals understand the Chinese language? Obviously not, although in simple situations a smooth exchange of symbols can be sustained. Problems begin to arise when ambiguities are encountered, due to situational exigencies. True understanding occurs, instead, when the rationale for linking symbols is grasped. In this way, the parameters of language use are not as inflexible, as when responses are predicated on the surface features of symbols. Novel situations can thus be handled with a sense of decorum. Language use, in other words, involves a pragmatic dimension that is missed when the empirical traits of symbols are the focus of attention.

As discussed in chapter 3, the idea that the transmission of information constitutes understanding is associated with the work of Shannon and Weaver.[23] According to their model, information is exchanged successfully when exact pieces of knowledge are transmitted without the noise, that is, random or unpredictable interference, resulting from interpretation. In Searle's example, this precision is achieved by having exchanges based on the empirical properties of Chinese characters. Hence there should be no doubt about which symbols belong together.

With regard to ELIZA and DOCTOR, the complete circuit necessary for input to be translated successfully into output is the product of a template. This end is accomplished in PLATO-DCS by accepting as universal the particular instructions that are used for advancing an argument. Precise categories are thus available for recognizing and channeling input; nothing is left to guesswork.

Realism is also at the basis of the discussions possible with SHRDLU. As mentioned earlier, an operator's instructions appear to be subject to evaluation because the knowledge base of this program is a host of interrelated symbols. Accordingly, reasoned rather than automatic responses to input appear to be generated. Any resulting interaction, nonetheless, is still contrived. The reason for this is quite simple. A particular subset of reason is assumed to be pivotal to interaction or created by the discourse. As with expert systems, a few scripts are adopted that contain the knowledge base, rules of logic, and goals necessary to interact competently.[24] Accordingly, the framework for representing knowledge is abstract and thus constitutes an absolute reality. Interaction does not occur because of the mutual recognition and acceptance of rules, but results from the imposition of a specific cognitive net.

In a rare critique, Colby questions the efficacy of computer therapists.[25] Language is viewed to be static in each of the interactive programs that has been discussed, and thus he charges that important elements of therapy are obscured. What he suggests is that speech should not be conceived as the sum of linguistic states. This is because language is infinitely complex, affect is concealed, nonverbal cues are omitted, and speech is decontextualized. These points are summarized nicely by some users of MORTON, when they write that this program "does not have the capability to interpret large amounts of free-form responses."[26] This destruction of language, in short, is thought to jeopardize the prospects for successful therapy. What has not been taken seriously by most of the members of the AI community is the research which indicates that language is not an object, structure, or some other inanimate phenomenon.

Yet defining language to be an object or structure has obvious advantages with regard to computerization. Language bits can be easily circumscribed and stored. Moreover, linguistic patterns can be identified and paired with others in a mechanistic manner, without any loss of meaning. Stated differently, template translations and reasoning conducted in terms of scripts are not recognized to be inherently problematic. For as long as the structural integrity of language is guaranteed, why should objections be raised? Dealing with the structure of language is not necessarily the key shortcoming of ELIZA and DOCTOR. Problems surface with these programs, instead, when interpretation is confronted. Therefore, the software packages that have been proposed to deal with speech are not necessarily natural language programs. They may have natural language front ends, but use of speech is still prescribed according to a standard code.[27]

## NATURAL LANGUAGE AND THERAPY

Contemporary theorists argue that language is not a structure, but an expressive medium. Rather than a structural net that somehow captures reality, speech is inextricably associated with how knowledge and order are portrayed. This is what Derrida means when he writes that expression does not defer to reality; language is not a surrogate for a more profound reality.[28] Therefore, he states, "nothing exists outside of the text."[29] What this declaration means to Jacques Lacan is that facts are derived from speech rather than reality. Reality is thus a linguistic habit.

What these newer commentators on the nature of language are announcing is the demise of dualism. Therefore, realism can no longer be viewed as an adequate method for describing the acquisition of knowledge. Knowledge cannot be thought to emanate from objects that are undefiled by interpretation, or be related to structural imperatives. Why is this the case? Simply put, all knowledge is understood to be mediated thoroughly by speech acts, and thus nothing emerges undefiled by language use. "Reality is the world we bespeak."[30] Roland Barthes agrees with this statement and writes that even objectivity is a special version of speech.[31] Hence, reality must emerge from the mélange of interpretations that compete to be accepted as representing valid norms.

Having language penetrate to the core of reality has posed problems for computer engineers and has hampered progress in the field of AI. Because reality cannot be approached as if it is obtrusive, the foundation of daily life is understood by these newer writers to be interpretive. What this suggests is that certain assumptions about correct demeanor are supposed to be accepted as valid by all informed or normal persons. Reality is not obtrusive, but is embedded within a variety of interpretations about how tasks get accomplished. Contrary to the claims made by Noam Chomsky, for instance, social competence is not the outgrowth of a "deep structure" or some other undefiled conceptual base.[32] Rather, as noted earlier, the generation of reality is an accomplishment, or an outcome that is not guaranteed. Winograd and Flores make this point when they state, "existence is interpretation, and interpretation is existence."[33]

Why does treating reality as a precarious entity pose such problems for software designers? Because knowledge, reason, and the rules of speech cannot be expected to be universally recognized. Common sense, in other words, has limited generalizability, due to the implied definitional character of reality. Accordingly, merely formalizing speech patterns provides no assurance that the resulting language will have any relevance. Instead, the way language is used in specific situations must guide the development of the protocol employed to simulate discourse. After all, discourse involves many layers of interpretation. Recognizing this limitation, however, restricts the techniques that sustain computerized interaction. In short, universal rules of cognition may never be outlined in exact terms. And thus, the scientific status of AI may be called into question; a prospect engineers associated with this field do not want to face.[34]

Clearly, giving primacy to common sense knowledge has implications for understanding dialogue. A reality is no longer available around which different viewpoints can coalesce. Therefore, emphasizing the exactness of information is insufficient to insure communication. Even template responses or scripts are embroiled within a web of interpretations that must be untangled. Merely guaranteeing that input and output will be matched with precision may be irrelevant in terms of the organization of interaction. Much more important, definitions of reality must be "fused," as Hans-Georg Gadamer says, before dialogue is possible.[35] And fusing reality assumptions is not at all similar to basing exchange on so-called objective referents.

Discourse is not necessarily the culmination of sending and receiving data. Information is interpreted before it is transmitted, and thus the influence of language use must be considered an essential part of the activity whereby knowledge is received. Barthes describes this sort of concern when he recommends that readers read in a manner similar to the way an author writes.[36] In this way, the world of an author can be entered and understood. Rapport is thus developed between a writer and reader.

Considering the linguistic nature of a client's existence, the same kind of empathy should be exhibited by a therapist. According to contemporary thinkers, only after entré has been gained to a client's world can dialogue begin. For interpersonal understanding occurs when the reality assumptions made by a client are apprehended, or when a client's "strategies of living and their consequences" are apprehended.[37] Therefore, the norms by which clients judge their actions can be known and included in a diagnosis. Social relevance thus becomes the theme that directs intervention.

Surely AI researchers must recognize that this kind of dialogue is different from information processing? Nonetheless, conveyed by programs such as ELIZA, SHRDLU, and PLATO-DCS is the idea that the transmission of knowledge is synonymous with understanding. And consistent with the views of Shannon and Weaver, clarity is thought to be improved as a consequence of increasing redundancy. In more concrete terms, more and more information is gathered. With regard to social service agencies, this means that the knowledge base of practitioners is expanded. Yet does this necessarily end in better understanding? Obviously not, for interpretation is not halted because additional data are available for evaluation; interpretation does not respect the presence of so-called objective data. Redundancy improves the likelihood of communication only when certainty can be equated with clarity. Yet when this conclusion is unwarranted, as is the case when language mediates communication, little may be gained from enlarging a knowledge base.

AI theorists have misconstrued the natural language problem. Rather than trying to constrain interpretation, they should study how language use affects interaction. But suggested by this new approach is that computers may have limited applicability to the simulation of therapy. Perhaps the verification of information that is vital to sustaining dialogue cannot be undertaken by a computer? For maintaining discourse is fraught with uncertainties, such as when reality assumptions are not reconfirmed as to whether or not they are still operational. The dynamism that is indigenous to dialogue, in other words, defies formalization. To pursue this course of action can only distort how dialogue actually proceeds. In short, practitioners may begin to think that dialogue occurs automatically following the accrual of a set amount of information. But, if the natural language problem is correctly understood, this conclusion should be reevaluated. Correspondingly, correct interpretation, rather than clarity, should be viewed as essential to understanding.

## CONCLUSION

Early on, Colby and his associates wrote that DOCTOR was unable to "offer interpretations based on a cognitive model of the person."[38] Nonetheless, this realization did not impede development of computerized therapists. At that time, however, one dissenting voice was heard. In conflict with mainstream opinion, Weizenbaum declared that computerized therapy was completely inappropriate and possibly obscene. In his debate with proponents of computer-mediated therapy, Weizenbaum points out that "respect, understanding, and love are not technical problems."[39] Accordingly, therapy should not be predicated on the mastery of technique. The human condition, instead, should be examined in order to discover the personal meaning and social significance of a problem, for only in this way will therapy be helpful.

The point raised by Weizenbaum relates to whether or not therapists are going to be "doctors of the soul," to use the phrase popularized by Viktor Frankl, or simply masters of technology.[40] Should clients be treated as objects, or be confirmed through the therapeutic relationship? Because language is now accepted to pervade reality, the latter course of action is the only one that seems feasible. Only through mutual understanding can the problems in living experienced by clients be solved, for these difficulties cannot be separated neatly from values and beliefs about the quality of a proper life.[41] In a similar vein, R.D. Laing writes that "persons are distinguished from things in that persons experience the world, whereas things behave in the world."[42] Nonetheless, natural language is regularly sacrificed in order to fulfill the requirements imposed by interactive programs such as DOCTOR and ELIZA. Thus, simply a caricature of a client is provided. Questions of technique, accordingly, come to obscure the *meaning* of a client's behavior; the spirit of language is systematically decimated.

Technical criteria are utilized to unite a client and therapist. If input falls within certain parameters, a specific output is produced. A client and therapist may confront each other as a result of this modus operandi, yet their respective viewpoints are not confirmed. They approach each other as objects. How can reasonable behavioral change be expected to result from this kind of therapeutic relationship? Although clients liked the anonymity provided by DOCTOR, they also felt frustrated by the responses given by this program.[43] Also, other research suggests that long-term change may not result from computerized discourse.[44] Forming an intimate therapeutic relationship may be risky, yet the benefits derived from this association seem to be far greater than those from interaction between a client and computer.

Clearly, the dimension of the interhuman is vital for successful therapy. Client and therapist, therefore, must each learn to "take the role of the other."[45] In other words, client and therapist must approach each other as fellow human beings, which is impossible with a computer. As might be suspected, computer-human interface based on technical improvements has little or nothing to do with this kind of intersubjectivity. The technical alignment of ego and alter must not be confused with real discourse, whereby the self-understanding of a client is penetrated. But once this insight is achieved, socially appropriate intervention can be proposed. In other words, a course of therapy that is consistent with a client's cognitive model can be developed.

Computerized therapy, however, consists of monologue. A real person is not encountered, but is a thoroughly abstract other. All responses are standardized, as well as the knowledge base that is supposed to explain a client's motives. In this way, the social character of health and illness is ignored. Practitioners should not be enticed by the technique of computerized therapy to the extent that the social side of intervention is ignored. The idea that therapy is based on successful interaction should never be overlooked. Otherwise, therapists will become nothing more than manipulators of the human condition. And obviously, manipulation is not the same as therapy. The metaphor of the computer, accordingly, is inappropriate for characterizing therapy.[46]

## NOTES

1. Harold P. Erdman, Melanie H. Klein, and John H. Greist, "Direct Patient Computer Interviewing," *Journal of Consulting and Clinical Psychology* 53(6) (1985): pp. 760-773.

2. Talcott Parsons, *The Social System* (New York: The Free Press, 1951), pp. 428ff.

3. Thomas Szasz, *Ideology and Insanity* (Garden City, NY: Doubleday, 1970), pp. 47, 53.

4. Joseph Weizenbaum, "ELIZA—A Computer Program for the Study of Natural Language Communication Between Man and Machine," *Communications of the Association For Computer Machinery* 9(1) (1966): pp. 36-45.

5. McCorduck, *Machines Who Think*, pp. 239-271.

6. Habermas, *Legitimation Crisis*, p. 108.

7. Weizenbaum, "ELIZA—A Computer Program" pp. 36-37

8. Kenneth M. Colby, James. B. Watt, and John P. Gilbert, "A Computer Method of Psychotherapy," *Journal of Nervous and Mental Disease* 142(2) (1966): pp. 148-152.

9. Joseph Weizenbaum, *Computer Power and Human Reason* (San Francisco: W. H. Freeman, 1976), p. 6.

10. Weizenbaum, ELIZA—Computer Program," p. 42

11. Philip DeMuth, "ELIZA and Her Offspring," in *Using Computers in Clinical Practice*, ed. Marc D. Schwartz (New York: The Haworth Press, 1984), pp. 321-327.

12. Ibid., pp. 321-322.

13. McCorduck, *Machines Who Think*, p. 255.

14. Yehoshua Bar-Hillel, "The Present Status of Automatic Translation of Languages," in *Advances in Computers*, vol. 1, ed. Franz L. Alt (New York: Academic Press, 1960), pp. 91-163.

15. Terry Winograd, "A Procedural Model of Language Understanding," in *Computer Models of Thought and Language*, ed. Roger C. Schank and Kenneth Mark Colby (San Francisco: W. H. Freeman, 1973), pp. 152-186.

16. Winograd, "Artificial Intelligence and Language Comprehension," p. 17.

17. John W. Murphy, "Deconstruction, Discourse, and Liberation," *Social Science Information* 26(2) (1987): pp. 417-433.

18. Winograd and Flores, *Understanding Computers and Cognition*, p. 121.

19. Werner Stark, *The Fundamental Forms of Social Thought* (New York: Fordham University Press, 1963), pp. 1-13.

20. Jacques Derrida, *Writing and Difference* (Chicago: University of Chicago Press, 1979), p. 34.

21. Morton Wagman, "PLATO-DCS: An Interactive Computer System for Personal Counseling," *Journal of Counseling Psychology* 27(1) (1980): pp. 16-30.

22. John R Searle, "Minds, Brains, Programs," in *Mind Design*, ed. John Haugeland (Cambridge: MIT Press, 1981), pp. 283-306.

23. McCorduck, *Machines Who Think*, p. 100.

24. Schank and Abelson, *Scripts, Plans, Goals, and Understanding*, pp. 36-68.

25. Kenneth M. Colby, "Computer Psychotherapists," in *Technology in Mental Health Care*, ed. Joseph B. Sidowski, James H. Jonson, and Thomas A. Williams (Norwood, NJ: Ablex, 1980), pp. 109-117.

26. Paulette Selmi, Marjorie H. Klein, John H. Greist, James H. Johnson, and William G. Harris, "An Investigation of Computer-Assisted Cognitive-Behavior Therapy in the Treatment of Depression," *Behavior Research Methods and Instrumentation* 14(2) (1982): pp. 181-185.

27. Heim, *Electric Language: A Philosophical Study of Word Processing*, pp. 82ff.

28. Jacques Derrida, *Speech and Phenomena* (Evanston: Northwestern University Press, 1973), pp. 48-59.

29. Jacques Derrida, *Of Grammatology* (Baltimore: The Johns Hopkins University Press, 1976), p. 158.

30. Heim, *Electric Language*, p. 30.

31. Roland Barthes, *The Rustle of Language* (New York: Hill and Wang, 1986), p. 160.

32. Noam Chomsky, *Aspects of the Theory of Syntax* (Cambridge: MIT Press, 1965), p. 136.

33. Winograd and Flores, *Understanding Computers and Cognition*, p. 31.

34. Dreyfus and Dreyfus, *Mind over Machine*, pp. 13-15.

35. Hans-Georg Gadamer, *Truth and Method* (New York: Crossroad, 1982), p. 273.

36. Roland Barthes, *Criticism and Truth* (Minneapolis: University of Minnesota Press, 1987), p. 69.

37. Szasz, *Ideology and Insanity*, p. 94.

38. Colby, Watt, and Gilbert, "A Computer Method of Psychotherapy," p. 151.

39. Weizenbaum, *Computer Power and Human Reason*, p. 270.

40. Viktor Frankl, *Doctor of the Soul* (New York: Knopf, 1966), p. x.

41. Szasz, *Ideology and Insanity*, pp. 19-24.

42. R.D. Laing, "The Mystification of Experience," in *Radical Psychology*, ed. Phil Brown (New York: Harper and Row, 1973), p. 114.

43. Colby, Watt, and Gilbert, "A Computer Method of Psychotherapy," p. 150.

44. Nolden, "Technology and Transference: Computers in Psychotherapy," pp. 67-75.

45. Herbert Blumer, *Symbolic Interactionism* (Englewood Cliffs, NJ: Prentice-Hall, 1969), pp. 78-89.

46. Dominic W. Massaro, "The Computer as a Metaphor for Psychological Inquiry: Considerations and Recommendations," *Behavior Research Methods, Instruments, and Computers* 18(2) (1986): pp. 73-92.

# 7

# Computerization and the Dehumanization of Human Services

## INTRODUCTION

Critics charge that the delivery of human services will be dehumanized as a result of computerization. The relationship between a patient and therapist may change, for example, along with other facets of treatment. Specifically, as has been suggested thus far, the human element may be pushed to the periphery of the intervention process, as technical requirements are given precedence over less technological considerations. Under the guise of improved rationality, all so-called subjective factors may be reduced in importance. Therefore, interpretation and experience will be eschewed as antagonistic to outlining a sensible plan for providing services.

Why would this démarche be tolerated? A brief look at the Western intellectual tradition is necessary to answer this question. As part of the general aim to objectify facts, mechanistic analogies have been adopted regularly to describe human functioning. Simply put, humans have been portrayed as operating in a machine-like fashion.[1] Szasz calls this process "mechanomorphism," when "modern man tries to understand man as if 'it' were a machine."[2] Describing persons in technical terms, therefore, should hardly be viewed as damaging. In fact, any other approach would be considered inappropriate.

Throughout early Western philosophy the relationship between the mind and body was treated as problematic.[3] In the work of Plato, for example, the mind was trapped within the body, thereby suggesting that these two elements are basically separate. Different from Plato, Aristotle argued that these two phenomena were linked, without adverse consequences to either one. During the medieval period, the same sort of equivocation is found, with the soul united to the body both directly and indirectly at different times. Not until Descartes' work was the association between the mind and the body clear. In fact, he offered the rationale that sustains much of modern psychology, particularly behavioral orientations.

From the discussion in chapter 2, Descartes should be seen as an advocate of dualism. Central to his project was dividing the world into two opposing components. These are *res extensa* and *res cogitans*. Hence, mental and bodily activities are restricted to different realms. Consequently, the body is transformed into an object—inanimate, passive, and available for examination. Actually, Descartes compared the body to a machine, for he assumed bodily functions were unaffected by consciousness.[4] La Mettrie, a French physician, took this position to an extreme and declared that the body operated according to laws of nature. Of course, many modern psychologists and psychiatrists would not necessarily quibble with La Mettrie's general orientation. The body, they might argue, is regulated by principles that are universal, readily measurable, and explainable in terms of the laws of physiology. Humans are thus no different from other natural phenomena. This trend is summarized nicely by Szasz when he states, "whereas primitive man personifies things, modern man 'thingifies' persons."[5] For example, the mind becomes the brain, cognition becomes information processing, and knowledge becomes input.

Because the mind is not obtrusive, as opposed to the brain, this component of existence is deemed to be inferior to more objective factors. The mind is assumed to be capricious and an unreliable source of information. Valid knowledge, therefore, must arrive from outside of the mind. At best, the mind is believed to be capable of recording reality. If the mind is properly controlled, a correct picture of reality can be obtained. Mimesis is the proper function of the mind. Thus human activity "serves to beautify and justify the established order."[6]

Using more psychological concepts, the mind is understood to respond to stimuli. A rudimentary form of this argument was advanced by philosophers such as Hobbes, Locke, and Hume.[7] According to them, the mind reacts to sense data, thus determining how persons will behave. Modern behaviorists have refined this viewpoint, and maintain that stimuli prompt persons into action. Hence, behavior should be explained with respect to a series of S → R statements. Moreover, as a result of the image of the mind conveyed by behaviorists, the search for the physiological mechanisms that are assumed to underpin cognition has been expedited. Research into the neural basis of mental activity has come to be viewed as extremely worthwhile. In point of fact, renewed interest in the neural net thesis has been expressed lately among scientists in the field of AI. According to this argument, the mind is nothing more than neural pathways—consisting of "simplified neurons and . . . [the] connections between them—that are periodically stimulated."[8]

As should be noted, using mechanistic and technological imagery to describe thinking is consistent with the mainstream of philosophy and psychology. Why then should the computerization of social services be understood as possibly dehumanizing? If humans are machines and merely respond to stimuli, why should the computer microworld be considered harmful? After all, humanization and dehumanization do not exist in a vacuum, but are constructs that have a historical context. And the traditional intellectual framework is not anathema to mechanistic renditions of knowledge and order.

Nonetheless, this trend has begun to change. With the onset of Kant, the mind was no longer considered to be passive.[9] Cognitive categories, instead, were understood to shape reality. This new tendency to view human action as intimately involved in shaping reality was furthered by Husserl, Heidegger, and a group of philosophers loosely known as existentialists. To use Husserl's terminology, all behavior is "intentional." "Consciousness," he writes, "is always consciousness of something."[10] What this means is that all knowledge, including scientific renditions of the mind and body, are mediated by human consciousness. Hence, knowledge is not objective in the Cartesian sense, but is socially constituted. Thus, humans are united inextricably to the generation of reality.

This change in describing humans is epitomized by a group of writers referred to as postmodernists. As noted in the previous chapter, these philosophers contend that all knowledge is derived from language games.[11] Their point is that reality is mediated by language use. Persons do not merely respond to stimuli, but through the exercise of language differentiate fact from fantasy. Rather than a neural state, knowledge emerges from a host of social processes. Instead of ancillary to reality, human action is at the core of existence. Nothing emerges undefiled by language; all knowledge stands in the midst of language. Thus, removing the body from the influence of interpretation is not a cogent maneuver.

Thus, persons should not be described in mechanistic terms. Their operation is much too complex for this sort of analysis. For example, definitions about reality provide the frame of reference that is used to organize daily life. Additionally, events are not stimuli, but factors that must be interpreted before they have any meaning. And the mind is not synonymous with the brain—the values, commitments, and beliefs that inundate reality cannot be reduced to bioelectrical reactions. In fact, the mind is a constellation of definitions persons adopt to orient and judge their behavior.[12]

In this regard, Arnold Gehlen contends that humans are not programmed at birth. Instead, he characterizes humans as suffering from "instinctual deprivation."[13] What this means is that the basic nature of humans is unstable and needs to be reinforced by social institutions, if individual continuity is to be attained. Hence, persons are not machines who have a fundamental nature. Through social action, or *praxis*, as Marxists say, human nature is created and continually recreated. Contrary to an inert object, human reality involves a "choice of being."[14] What this shift in thinking announces to postmodernists is the death of man, because, as Roland Barthes notes, the "I is nothing other than the instance of saying I."[15] Hence, language use seeps even into the deepest recesses of human existence and renders a person's identity fluid and always open to change.

Therefore, any attempt to obscure the influence of human action should be considered dehumanizing, according to these new standards. Eliminating interpretation from the discovery and analysis of data, in other words, should be viewed as reductionistic. Further, describing social phenomena in technical terms should be understood to undermine important interpretive considerations pertaining to knowledge and order. Stated differently, the social basis of knowledge, language, and rationality, for example, may be seriously misconstrued if these items are handled in this way.

Due to the linguistic basis of reality, what criterion exists for criticizing computerization? After all, computerization is simply another form of language. The key problem with computerization is that all other conceptions of reality are dismissed as unimportant by this rendition of reasoning. As a result, actual expressions are viewed sympathetically only when they conform to the strictures imposed by computerization. In this discussion, such reductionism is considered to be dehumanizing.

The aim of this chapter is not to defend the existence of genetic or other primeval traits that are supposed to be indicative of humanness. Instead, in view of recent theoretical advances, what is human can be revealed only through the various modes of expression persons choose to enact. What needs to be protected in the name of humanism, therefore, is the polyvalent character of personal and social action.

## ELEMENTS OF DEHUMANIZATION

### Facts

Within the computer microworld facts are assumed to have a unique form. As is explained in chapter 2, digitalization is central to the process of separating fact from opinion.[16] Information that can be operationalized as a bit is considered to be valuable, while other forms of knowledge are regarded as purely speculative.

Portraying knowledge in this way, however, is potentially dehumanizing. Why? Suggested by the imagery of the information bit is that knowledge is a thing. Valuable data are translated into quantities of information, as is indicated by the binary logic used to create bits.[17] Hence, valid knowledge is unambiguous. Stated differently, facts are clear and concise. Yet striving for clarity in this way may be very problematic.

By placing knowledge in the pristine space provided by computerization, the image is created that knowledge can be externalized. In a dualistic fashion, information is placed in a context that neutralizes data. Knowledge is thus objectified, or apparently divorced from situational contingencies. Additionally, and in a very subtle way, this decontextualization of facts begins to redefine the human condition. Rather than existing *in situ*, knowledge is disassociated from considerations that would limit its generalizability. Foucault describes the outcome of this process by claiming that the human gaze is "mathematized."[18]

Facts are stripped of their symbolic value. The idea that a piece of information may be polysemic is given little credence; each datum is assumed to have a single identity.[19] For due to the emphasis placed on binary logic, the undecidables—elements that defy simple classification—that are indigenous to the social constitution of knowledge are overlooked. The idea that facts have to be preserved in the midst of a mélange of competing symbols, or interpretations, is not recognized.

What does this rendition of facts imply about truth? Specifically, truth is thought to be conveyed adequately by a copy theory of knowledge. The usual way of expressing this thesis is *adaequatio rei et intellectus*.[20] Two propositions are important at this juncture. First, an object is presumed to exist that is undefiled by interpretation; second, when this referent is reflected by the mind, truth is acquired. In this sense, truth is waiting to be revealed by those who are able to overcome their illusions. Those who can transcend the restrictions imposed by subjectivity are placed in close proximity to absolute knowledge.

This definition of truth, however, is inconsistent with more modern renditions proposed by Heidegger[21] and J. Hillis Miller.[22] They have argued, respectively, that truth should be understood as *aletheia* or as *mise en abîme*. Their point, as is suggested by the term *aletheia*, is that truth is concealed beneath layers of existence. Symbolism, in other words, is not diaphanous but dense. In this sense, acquiring truth is the result of a process whereby a particular rendition of symbolism is given primacy over others. "Truth," as Lyotard says, "doesn't speak, *stricto sensu*; it works."[23] Hence, truth remains unconcealed until a clearing can be created that will separate, at least momentarily, competing definitions of reality. Accordingly, Barthes writes that even "evident truths are . . . only choices;" truths are "already interpretations."[24]

Treating facts as if they are bits is considered to be dehumanizing for a simple reason: the creative capacity of persons is dismissed as insignificant in the discovery of facts. The role played by human action in establishing the conditions to determine valid knowledge is curtailed. Presumed is that persons merely encounter facts, classify these bits of information, and respond in a manner that is deemed to be socially correct. And due to the prominence given to realism, reflecting reality is believed to be indicative of rational behavior. That individuals do not react to facts, but respond to the *meaning* of events that is socially constituted, is not considered to be a noteworthy finding.

## Language Use

One of the major problems facing those who want to computerize aspects of social life relates to how language is used by persons in their everyday affairs.[25] As is illustrated in chapter 6, before the therapeutic relationship could be computerized, the way clients use language to define themselves, their behavior, and their surroundings must be rendered programmable. If this is not done, how can computers be expected to interact properly with patients or therapists? And unless the beliefs, values, and commitments exhibited by persons can be built into software, how can the interface between computers and humans ever be effective?

Marvin Minsky, along with a gaggle of other writers, refer to this as the "frame problem."[26] What is acknowledged by this idea is that humans do not necessarily reside in a world comprised of empirical indices. In other words, while organizing their daily activities persons are not limited to manipulating objects and responding to stimuli. Instead, judgments are made that are based on assumptions about the nature of reality. These presuppositions, moreover, constitute the stock of knowledge that is consulted when the need arises to distinguish normal from abnormal behavior.[27] Through language use and other cognitive means a pool of information is maintained that serves to rationalize a person's actions. This body of knowledge relates to the "human, temporal, situated, continuously changing know-how" that sustains interaction among the members of a particular community.[28]

Computers will respond haphazardly to social situations unless these assumptions, or "recipes," are introduced into programs. The cognitive or linguistic categories that are used to construct reality must be replicated in the form of command statements or the nuances of social interaction will be obscured. Whoever thought computer technicians would have to become epistemologists, in order for advances to be made in computer science? Nonetheless, those who undertake the task of constructing knowledge bases for computer software should begin to rethink perennial philosophical questions that pertain to the connection between facts and values. For as philosophers have always argued, moral and technical issues cannot be conveniently separated, even in a high-tech world.

That computer scientists should recognize the importance of language is encouraging. Yet the way in which language has been conceived has serious shortcomings. Specifically, language is believed to consist of basic structures that are linked together.[29] Language is assumed to consist of morphemes, phonemes, and syntax, which are organized properly by competent speakers. This portrayal of language allows natural speech patterns to be adjusted to the rigid categories used in computerizing knowledge, with no appreciable distortion. After all, structures are relatively easily replicated. As a result of the emphasis that is placed on maintaining structural integrity, however, communicative competence becomes synonymous with classifying events similarly. But as noted earlier in the discussion of the natural language problem, the pragmatic thrust of language is obscured by the structural rendition of language.

Persons are entrapped within language when it is understood to be a structural apparatus. Overlooked is that language is not static, but a process that is always changing. Instead of being restricted by structural mandates, language is constantly expanding. Accordingly, Merleau-Ponty remarks that when someone speaks, both more and less than was originally intended is expressed, because a "halo of signification" accompanies every linguistic act.[30] Because events are given meaning by language, rather than simply classified, the dominance of specific linguistic acts is never guaranteed. Due to the fluidity of language, referred to by Barthes as the "excess of the signifier," the boundaries of speech are routinely transgressed and new definitions of reality emerge and gain acceptance.[31] Those who oppose structuralist versions of language claim that speech can never be completely stabilized because of its creative nature.

Minimized by a structural characterization of language is the inventiveness of speech. As a consequence, the norms for determining health, illness, sanity, and madness, for example, are not recognized to be a product of linguistic conventions. Obviously, ignoring this creative side of speech has undesirable consequences, particularly in terms of understanding how persons explain their behavior. Specifically important, ignoring the linguistic basis of knowledge can culminate in practitioners never truly understanding their clients. In this regard, clients are not sensitively treated.

### Reason or Rationality

Key to the appeal of computers is their alleged rationality. Any activity that is computerized is believed to become increasingly rational, because instructions are faithfully followed, events are reliably classified, and decisions are rendered without disruption. Procedures are executed, in other words, without much equivocation and thus error. Once proper response protocol have been identified, input and output are easily matched. Hence, surprises are kept to a minimum.

Through the use of formal logic, the ratio between input and output is maximized. The resulting improvements in efficiency are witnessed because uncertainty is removed from decision making. Consistent with the demands of formal logic, mutually exclusive response categories are implemented, step-by-step instructions are employed for identifying events, and a single format for deriving conclusions is established. As some critics have stated, achieving increased rationality in this case is predicated on restricting cognition to elementary types of activities. Any deviation from standardized response sets, in other words, is not tolerated.

As should be noticed, the definition of reason that sustains computerization equates consistency with rationality. Of course, formalization will reduce the number of unexpected occurrences, yet reason is eviscerated in the process. Is rationality nothing more than the ability to follow instructions, compare facts, and draw conclusions from premises? Various AI researchers argue that this version of reason misses a very important point.[32] That is, the ability to learn is a vital component of rational behavior.

In this context, learning is understood much more broadly than it is in behavioral theories. Implied is that persons are able to recognize and adapt to any special circumstances which may be unexpected in a situation. Further, that rules may not have universal applicability is also appreciated. Rationality, in short, is exhibited when persons apprehend the limited nature of reality assumptions, understand the context of the rules used for decision making, and recognize that a circuitous route may be followed when reaching conclusions. To paraphrase René Thom, the characteristics of reason are "locally determined."[33] Reason is a manifestation of the task environment in which behavior is enacted, along with the way this setting is interpreted and altered through further interaction.[34]

When reason is formalized, the many ways in which rationality is expressed go unexamined. Additionally, little attention is devoted to reviewing the activity whereby premises are legitimized. Humans are treated as if they are merely problem solvers. What this means, according to Newell and Simon, is that particular information is available to informed and rational persons: knowledge pertaining to "what is desired, under what conditions, by means of what tools and operations, starting with what initial information, and with access to what resources."[35] Yet the process of decision making is seldom this clearly outlined; all the facets of making a rational choice are rarely this clear cut and divorced from situational exigencies.

Because premises are based on interpretation and are not necessarily omnipresent, reason and consistency should not be viewed as similar. In postmodern parlance, rationality "begins and ends with conceptualization," claims Derrida. Thus, the logic of decision making can be assessed only when the situational relevance of premises is incorporated into the procedures used by practitioners to evaluate behavior.[36] Consistency, at best, is indirectly related to relevance, for irrelevant premises may lead consistently to conclusions that are socially meaningless. What this means is that defining reason is a social rather than a logistical matter.

As described by ethnomethodologists, reason is an accomplishment.[37] Particular premises are advanced that are corroborated sometimes by a wide range of persons. Through a variety of techniques, known as etc. procedures, premises that are accepted are continually reinforced. In this way, presuppositions that are basically contingent are reaffirmed and kept from slipping into obscurity. This is what he means when Heidegger declares that truth is an event, or something that is appropriated, rather than something which is obvious.[38] Accordingly, the premises that are at the heart of reason must be reviewed regularly, so as to insure that they are still operative. Again, the point is that reason is constructed through interaction and is extremely variable. Failure to notice these variations may mean that a client's behavior will be misrepresented.

## HOW MAY THESE THEORETICAL CONSIDERATIONS FACILITATE DEHUMANIZATION?

### Search for Data

As a result of the conception of facts associated with computerization, the kinds of information that are collected may be adversely affected. After all, data are supposed to be empirical, objective, and comparable to information bits. Knowledge that does not conform to these expectations may be avoided or disregarded altogether. The emphasis that is placed on quantification, in other words, may begin to dictate how the search for information proceeds. Winner refers to this process as reverse adaptation, because the outcome is "the adjustment of human ends to match the character of the available means."[39]

The activity of garnering data can be altered in a variety of ways. First the distinction between so-called hard and soft data may be accepted unquestioningly. When this occurs, preference is usually given to methodologies that appear to be uninfluenced by interpretation. Data derived from fixed-format questionnaires or input forms, for example, may be deemed more valuable than information gained from interviews. These instruments may be viewed as capable of producing reliable data because interaction between researchers and respondents is minimized.

Second, the sentiments expressed by research subjects or clients may not be treated as valuable, unless these claims can be corroborated by some sort of objective measure. A patient's complaints may be ignored, until they are proven to have an empirical basis. As a result, laboratory tests or other technical means may come to be used regularly to verify whether or not a client's descriptions of his or her symptoms are factual.[40] So-called subjective judgments must not be allowed to cloud the facts of a case.

And third, information that cannot be transformed into a bit and prepared easily for data processing may be underutilized. Data processing requirements, as is suggested by Winner, may begin to surreptitiously influence how data are chosen. Nowadays this problem is particularly prevalent due to the widespread use of computers in agencies to store the records of clients and other regularly used information. Due to the proliferation of standardized forms, data that cannot be readily adapted to these instruments may be dismissed as bothersome. These more elaborate data may be designated as vague or ambiguous and excluded from knowledge bases.

Due to the importance given to data with exact parameters, information that appears unclear may be given a low priority. This means that a host of information sources will never be consulted. Subtly, and not so subtly, the search for facts will be truncated, thereby excluding various realms of experience from client assessments. Evaluation, for example, may become equated with testing, because this format appears to exclude the influence of subjectivity. Too bad that empirical indices are often unrelated to how events are socially constructed! Yet to recognize the social construction of facts is often understood to undermine data collection. Therefore, interpretation is sacrificed in order to obtain precise data.

### The Stabilization of Concepts

The formalization of language required by computerization also has substantial negative side effects. In short, similar to the aims of the members of the Vienna Circle, language use is gradually refined to the extent that very exact concepts are available.[41] Obtaining this degree of precision, however, requires that language be defined in behavioral terms. Hence, concepts are operationalized with regard to readily observable markers. As a result, goals, objectives, and other reliable measures can be formulated for both managerial and clinical purposes.

For example, management by objectives (MBO) has gained increased popularity in social service agencies, as a by-product of the move to increased computerization. Actually, MBO was created during the 1950s to make management scientific. This feat was to be accomplished through the incorporation of cybernetic theory into the operation of organizations.[42] The thrust of this approach is to eliminate opinions and other sources of bias from the evaluation of job performance. Therefore, so-called objective indicators, or bench marks, are employed to assess whether or not performance goals are reached. In order to create the illusion that subjectivity is not a part of this process, concepts are equated with easily measurable behaviors. Acceptance of services, which is a very elusive notion, may be shown by clients rarely missing their medication or counseling sessions. Rendering goals concrete in this way is thought to upgrade the management of service agencies, and thus better treatment is presumed to be offered to clients.

This formalization of language is also currently witnessed in the development of treatment plans. In this case, the anticipated results of treatment are outlined in very restricted language. What are sometimes called weasel terms are thus supposed to be purged from treatment plans; nothing but positively worded and objectively measurable statements are supposed to be used. Difficult notions such as self-esteem and self-concept must be translated into precise levels of measurement. Improved personal hygiene, for instance, is often cited to be indicative of increased self-esteem. Articulating goals in this way is thought to enhance the detection of behavioral change.

Undermining research and knowledge-based interventions is not the desired result of this critique. Certainly, clearly defined measures of treatment success should replace the vague ideas that have guided intervention for years. Nonetheless, as most practitioners have experienced, restricting goal development to the use of traditionally defined empirical indices may mean that only the simplest problems will be addressed. Because personal hygiene factors and managerial processes are easy to measure, these considerations may be singled out regularly for attention. Simply, the impression is conveyed by the desire to formalize language that more complex issues cannot or, possibly, should not be tackled. For within the confines of behavioral language, only a limited range of indicators has validity.

Practitioners should remember that the formalization of language is justified by a specific, and thus limited, epistemology. Although knowledge can be conceptualized in many ways, key to the success of formalization is that technical criteria be used to differentiate fact from opinion. Thus, for the most part, conceptualization is bound to goals that reflect traditional empirical indicators. Objectives that diverge from this epistemology may be viewed with suspicion and discarded. Cognitive and emotional issues, for instance, appear to be difficult to formalize and may be regularly downplayed.

### Decision Making

The purpose of formal logic is to establish an archetype of the reasoning process. By doing this, the belief is that situational limitations can be overcome and universal explanations of behavior can be forthcoming. Due to the abstract nature of both premises and the rules for deriving conclusions, reasoning that is devoid of human foibles is now thought to be possible. Reasoning as it is supposed to exist can be inaugurated, because values and other sources of prejudice can be purged from the decision-making process. As remarked by Foucault, hollow spaces are available for use in constructing arguments; nonutilitarian places provide a safe environment for testing judgments.[43]

In clinical practice, this tendency to idealize decision making is revealed in the drive to computerize diagnoses. As might be expected, concordance among evaluators is believed to be greatly improved as a result of this maneuver, because premises are thought to lead naturally to conclusions when logic is formalized. And due to branching capabilities that can be built into software packages, the number of clinical instruments that can be administered via computers is increasing almost daily.[44]

In this way, decision making is rendered routine, because so-called nonrational considerations do not have a role to play in this process. As a result, clinical insight may be replaced by explicitly delineated protocol for diagnosing a problem, while procedural rigor is substituted for experience. Yet will this shift cause clinical skills to atrophy? After all, making a diagnosis will entail simply reading computer tapes and other instruments. Judgments may thus be made with little attention given to unique patterns of symptoms, for all that really matters is a final score or profile.[45] The contingencies that can produce variations in subscales may be viewed eventually as a nuisance, for the generalizability of diagnoses will be reduced.

Most important, the logic trees on which diagnostic schemes such as the DSM-III are based omit the values that sustain premises. As a result, reason and reasonableness are not distinguished. But according to Chaim Perelman, decisions may be rational but thoroughly unreasonable.[46] Understanding that certain conclusions may be justified is certainly rational, yet these final judgments may be socially irrelevant or lack reasonableness. But when diagnoses are not reasonable, symptoms and complaints can be easily be misconstrued by rational indices. When this is the case, an enormous amount of damage can be done in the name of rationality. Yet rational but harmful diagnoses may not be challenged, because of their alleged scientific stature.

## CONCLUSION

Computers can become dehumanizing because of reductionism. This tendency to equate knowledge, language, and reason with a few obvious empirical indicators may have been justified in the past, yet this position is unacceptable in view of newer theories. Recent philosophical shifts have rendered obsolete the idea that persons are machines which merely classify input and respond to stimuli. Persons are more complex than is revealed by this portrayal.

Through interaction persons define their environment, with respect to determining what is factual and real. Therefore, to use the distinction made by Ludwig Binswanger, practitioners should no longer be concerned with normalcy but health.[47] Standards of normalcy are defunct, in other words, because of the pragmatic character of reality. Health is an experiential notion that requires holistic analysis, whereas normalcy is empirical and can be easily ascertained. What is most dehumanizing about computerization is that knowledge, language, and reason are decontextualized and systematically disconnected from the imperfect discourse that is integral to defining health. Daily interaction is not perfect because truth is attained only indirectly, or by understanding the interrelationship among conceptions of reality.

As a result of computerization, one style of knowledge, language, and reason is elevated above all others. Furthermore, how the premises of one conceptual scheme may violate the presupposition of other definitions of reality is ignored. As a result, practitioners may begin to disregard how their diagnosis categories misconstrue the cognitive maps of the clients that are served. As Foucault indicates, the bipolarity of the normal and pathological may be routinely accepted.[48] Nonetheless, unless the experiential dimension of health is grasped, how can appropriate interventions be planned? At best, an idealized human being with typical problems will be encountered. And treatment that is predicated on such an outlook can hardly be therapeutic.

## NOTES

1. Harold E. Hatt, *Cybernetics and the Image of Man* (Nashville: Abington Press, 1968), pp. 23-50.

2. Szasz, *Ideology and Insanity*, p. 199.

3. Paul Ricoeur, *Fallible Man* (New York: Fordham University Press, 1986), pp. 81-132

4. Susan Bordo, *The Flight to Objectivity* (Albany: State University Press of New York, 1987), pp. 88-95.

5. Szasz, *Ideology and Insanity*, p. 199.

6. Herbert Marcuse, *Counterrevolution and Revolt* (Boston: Beacon Press, 1972), p. 92.

7. Samuel Enoch Stumpf, *Socrates to Sartre* (New York: McGraw-Hill, 1966), pp. 236-238, 272-299.

8. Margaret A. Boden, *Minds and Mechanisms: Philosophical Psychology and Computational Models* (Ithaca: Cornell University Press, 1981), pp. 89-112.

9. Joseph F. Rychlak, *A Philosophy of Science for Personality Theory* (Boston: Houghton Mifflin, 1968), pp. 278-283.

10. Edmund Husserl, *Paris Lectures* (The Hague: Nijhoff, 1975), p. 13.

11. Lyotard, *The Postmodern Condition*, p. 10.

12. Michel Foucault, "What Is An Author?" in *Textual Strategies*, ed. Josue V. Harari (Ithaca: Cornell University Press, 1979), pp. 141-160.

13. Arnold Gehlen, *Man in the Age of Technology* (New York: Columbia University Press, 1980), pp. 2-3.

14. Jean-Paul Sartre, *Existential Psychoanalysis* (Chicago: Gateway, 1969), p. 123.

15. Roland Barthes, *Image, Music, Text* (New York: Hill and Wang, 1977), p. 145.

16. Felix Guattari, *Molecular Revolution* (New York: Penguin Books, 1984), pp. 163-172.

17. Lyotard, *The Postmodern Condition*, p. 4.

18. Michel Foucault, *The Birth of the Clinic* (New York: Random House, 1975), p. 13.

19. John W. Murphy, "Foucault's Ground of History," *International Philosophical Quarterly* 24(2) (1984): pp. 189-196.

20. Walter Biemel, *Martin Heidegger* (New York: Harcourt Brace Jovanovich, 1976), pp. 61-66.

21. Martin Heidegger, *Being and Time* (New York: Harper and Brothers, 1962), pp. 262ff.

22. J. Hillis Miller, "Stevens' Rock and Criticism as Cure," *Georgia Review* 30(1) (1976): pp. 5-31.

23. Jean-Francois Lyotard, *Driftworks* (New York: Semiotext(e), 1984), p. 35.

24. Barthes, *Criticism and Truth*, p. 39.

25. Earl B. Hunt, *Artificial Intelligence* (New York: Academic Press, 1975), pp. 409-439.

26. Marvin Minsky, "A Framework for Representing Knowledge," in *Mind Design*, ed. John Haugeland (Montgomery, VT: Bradford Books, 1981), pp. 95-128; Hubert L. Dreyfus, "A Framework for Misrepresenting Knowledge," in *Philosophical Perspectives in Artificial Intelligence*, ed. Martin Ringle (Atlantic Highlands, NJ: Humanities Press, 1979), pp. 124-136.

27. Alfred Schutz, *Collected Papers* 2 (The Hague: Nijhoff, 1964), pp. 29-35.

28. Dreyfus and Dreyfus, *Mind over Machine*, p. 82.

29. Winograd, *Understanding Natural Language*, pp. 16-23; Steven C. Shwartz, *Applied Natural Language Processing* (Princeton, NJ: Petrocelli Books, 1987), pp. 21-56.

30. Maurice Merleau-Ponty, *The Visible and the Invisible* (Evanston, Il: Northwestern University Press, 1968), pp. 96-97.

31. Barthes, *The Rustle of Language*, p. 198.

32. Daniel Dennett, "Cognitive Wheels: The Frame Problem of AI," pp. 129-151.

33. Lyotard, *The Postmodern Condition*, p. 61.

34. Winograd and Flores, *Understanding Computers and Cognition*, pp. 22-23.

35. Thomas D. McFarland and Reese Parker, *Expert Systems in Education and Training* (Englewood Cliffs, NJ: Educational Technology Publications, 1990), p. 47.

36. Jacques Derrida, *Dissemination* (Chicago: University of Chicago Press, 1981), p. 19.

37. Kenneth Leiter, *A Primer On Ethnomethodology* (New York: Oxford University Press, 1980), pp. 97-105, 107-116.

38. Heidegger, *Being and Time*, pp. 253ff.

39. Winner, *Autonomous Technology*, p. 229.

40. John W. Murphy and Joseph J. Pilotta, "Some Epistemological Issues Related to Using the Medical Record for Organizational Decision Making,"

in *Qualitative Methodology, Theory and Application*, ed. John W. Murphy and Joseph J. Pilotta (Dubuque, IA: Kendall/Hunt, 1983), pp. 139-155.

41. Victor Kraft, *The Vienna Circle* (New York: The Philosophical Library, 1953).

42. Dale D. McConkey, *Management by Objectives for Non-Profit Organizations* (New York: AMA, 1975).

43. Foucault, *The Birth of the Clinic*, pp. 3-21.

44. Harold P. Erdman and Sharon W. Foster, "Computer-Assisted Assessment with Couples and Families," *Family Therapy* 13(1) (1986): pp. 23-40.

45. Matarazzo, "Computerized Test Interpretation: Unvalidated Plus All Mean and No Sigma," pp. 41-46.

46. Chaim Perelman, *The New Rhetoric and The Humanities* (Dordrecht: D. Reidel Publishing, 1979), pp. 117-123.

47. Ludwig Binswanger, *Being-in-the-World* (New York: Basic Books, 1963), pp. 206-221.

48. Foucault, *The Birth of the Clinic*, p. 35.

# 8

# Ethical Issues Related to Computerized Service Delivery

## INTRODUCTION

The idea that patients have rights is relatively new. Even during the early 1900s, clients who entered treatment were not given humane care.[1] Because social and psychological problems were not well understood, both physical and mental cruelty were commonplace. Often clients were placed in a treatment facility to receive custodial care and, for all practical purposes, forgotten. Although reformers in the nineteenth and early twentieth century attempted to change the horrendous conditions encountered by clients, even as recent as the late 1950s, treatment programs in the United States and elsewhere were a disgrace.[2]

During the 1950s evidence suggested that little therapy was actually occurring in treatment facilities. In fact, state hospitals were identified as very dangerous places. In less dramatic terms, confinement was the key treatment modality. Facilities were overcrowded, and thus only those who were wealthy could be guaranteed adequate care.[3] Accordingly, clients did not necessarily have the right to treatment, let alone freedom from cruel and unusual practices. Behavioral classifications were crude or nonexistent, monitoring was haphazard, and the goals of treatment were unclear.

As a result, the thrust of placement was social control; those who exhibited adjustment problems were simply kept out of public view. The use of tranquilizing drugs, electroshock, and psychosurgery made this task relatively easy.

As demonstrated by Erving Goffman, treatment facilities had become "total institutions."[4] Every aspect of a client's life was regulated, although therapy was not involved in this process. All that occurred was patients learned to adapt to the demands made by clinicians and administrators. Indeed, the terms "institutional neurosis" and "hospitalism" were coined to describe the passive and dependent behavior clients were expected to exhibit.[5] Deprived of their dignity, patients adjusted to the repressive norms enacted in treatment facilities and eventually could not function outside of these institutions. Those who were served were gradually debilitated—"disculturated," as Sommer stated—for restraint and security were the focus of concern.[6]

In the early 1960s, a concerted effort was made to upgrade these conditions. As mentioned in chapter 2, President Kennedy inaugurated what is commonly referred to as the community mental health movement. This new approach was designed to insure humane treatment for those with behavioral or psychological disorders.[7] For example, placements were to be made in the "least restrictive environment," rather than simply asylums. Moreover, individualized treatment plans that were reviewed regularly were to be utilized. And perhaps most important, patients were given the right to refuse treatment, and to be fully informed about every course of clinical action. Clients were now understood to be consumers who had a vital role to play in their rehabilitation. Subsequently, the usual practices had to be altered when prescribing treatment alternatives. Especially significant is that the entire therapeutic endeavor had to be subject to public scrutiny. No longer could therapy be undertaken without informed consent on the part of clients.

A good deal of experimentation was inaugurated at this time. Community mental health centers (CHMCs) were built to supply an alternative to long-term, in-patient treatment. Moreover, intervention was supposed to be client-centered, rather than designed to meet the criteria set by the medical profession. Halfway houses, family care projects, and other novel modes of therapy were tried, which were proposed to develop social skills on the part of clients. In general, the community setting was understood to be the most viable place to begin addressing social problems such as mental illness.[8] And accompanying this shift away from the medical model was supposed to be an increase in the dignity accorded to clients. Stated differently, the value-base of a community should become instrumental in defining the key issues related to treatment.

## COMPUTER TECHNOLOGY AND TREATMENT

Most important at this juncture is whether or not the introduction of computer technology will lessen the impact of the landmark 1963 legislation, which mandates that programs "should . . . serve as facilitators for clients' identification, definition, development, and expansion of their personal cognitive and emotional resources."[9] For example, will patients be moved to the periphery of the treatment process, due to the use of computers by clinicians and other practitioners? There is good reason to suspect that a whole new range of ethical issues will be broached because of the presence of this technology. The purpose of this chapter is to discuss a variety of these developments, in order to avoid returning to the days when patients had little to say about the ways in which they were handled.

Due to certain conceptual flaws, clients can be easily dehumanized through the use of computers. As was discussed in the previous chapter, the social imagery that is conveyed portrays existence in material terms, including human beings, and thus values, beliefs, and commitments are dismissed as unimportant in the planning, implementation, and evaluation of an intervention. Accordingly, the formalization that is attendant to computerization may extend into the domain of ethics. Due to the presence of computers the way in which clients are approached in social service organizations may be irremediably and negatively altered, unless direct and decisive corrective action is taken. In this sense, the impact of computerization must not be permitted to obscure the rights of clients to appropriate treatment. The logistics of computerization, in other words, must not begin to dictate organizational behavior. Kept in mind should be the understanding that intervention must be community based in the era of community or deinstitutionalized service delivery.

**Exclusion from Therapy**

Functional, biomedical, and ecological models are no longer supposed to be used when making diagnoses and organizing other types of intervention. These approaches are considered to be reductionistic, because the human element is believed to be ancillary to the requirements imposed by the social system. In this way, deviance and illness are not envisioned to have interpretive significance, but meaning that is derived from abstract and natural sources. Social problems are thus medicalized, claims Ivan Illich.[10] What this means is that client-oriented intervention is not undertaken; instead, the views of clients are treated as inferior to other, more scientific types of knowledge.

Psychological or behavioral problems are thought to be caused by physical factors. Psychologists and physicians, moreover, are empowered to discover these variables and formulate remedies.[11] As a result, patient input tends to be minimized, relative to the data that are found in official records. Additionally, laboratory tests and other scientific means are given priority when formulating clinical judgments. In the end, clients are moved to the periphery of the intervention process.

During the 1960s, the exalted status of medical practitioners and other professionals was seriously questioned. The insensitivity and biases concealed by diagnostic schemes were brought to public attention by the so-called anti-psychiatry movement.[12] Accordingly, physicians were illustrated to harbor negative opinions about the members of certain social classes, in addition to women and minority groups. Often these clients were approached as if they could not benefit from real treatment, but only custodial care. Nonetheless, these prejudices were exposed and were supposed to be rejected by community mental health workers. As a consequence of abandoning the medical model of illness in favor of more culturally sensitive conceptual frameworks, the ways in which clients and communities interpret themselves is elevated in importance. The significance of medical input is reduced, while the sentiments expressed by clients are increased in value.

Yet this trend may be reversed because of the introduction of computers into the clinical setting. The purpose for adopting these machines is problematic: the use of these instruments is believed to guarantee improved inter-rated reliability.[13] Because computers are unaffected by situational exigencies, clinical judgments can be predicated on objective evidence. Essentially the role of computers is to reinforce measurement and classificatory processes that would otherwise be haphazard. Again, the assumption is made that particular types of information are inherently worth more than others. Most troublesome, however, is that technical experts will most likely have sole access to these devices. And because these specialists are viewed to possess unique and powerful knowledge, they may begin to occupy the central position on a treatment team. Dery expresses this sentiment nicely when he states that programmers "create a whole data base out of zeros and ones, but then they are the only ones who can pull data out in a way that you and I can read it."[14] Therefore, clients may be systematically excluded from the development of their treatment plans and other intervention activities.

Yet what about the provision that all assessment protocol and clinical activities must be subject to public review? A small coterie of technicians can easily begin to dominate a social service agency, once computers are introduced. Treatment facilities, in other words, may come to be run by technocrats. As tasks become more complex and based on technical requirements, the knowledge possessed by technicians becomes increasingly valuable. As Winner writes, "the need for planning, coordination, and comprehension ... make[s] the technical aristocracy necessary."[15] Hence, the insight offered by clients and members of the community begins to appear insignificant. Accordingly, care must be taken to insure that practitioners do not become so enamored of technique that treatment falls within the sole purview of technical experts. For if this is the case, the participation of the public in this process may be seriously curtailed.

## Technology as Ideology

The straitjacket is no longer thought to supply viable imagery for describing treatment. For resurrected are conceptions of therapy that are hardly complimentary. In fact, nowadays clients must be guaranteed freedom from the coercion that can result when they are not given the opportunity to participate directly in any intervention that is undertaken. Moreover, implied by the idea of participation is that patients can refuse treatment and critique any procedure. Critical self-evaluation and autonomy are now considered to be essential components of a truly therapeutic setting.[16] But clients may submit willingly to the wishes of a practitioner because of the position in which they find themselves. Accordingly, the computerization of services should not aggravate this situation.

Can one result of computerization be that the freedom of clients is placed in jeopardy? At this time, numerous writers charge that technology can be transformed easily into a repressive ideology.[17] Herbert Marcuse, for example, states that " . . . in the medium of technology, man and nature become fungible objects of organization."[18] Their point is that technology can stifle critical inquiry, and thus facilitate the establishment of an asymmetrical or manipulative relationship between a client and therapist. Clearly, tolerating this subtle use of power violates the spirit of the clients' rights movement.

Why is technology an ideology? Simply put, because computers operate on the basis of a standardized format, the illusion can be perpetrated that any computerized activity is automatically value-free. Therefore, computerized knowledge is treated as unquestionably objective and valid. As with ideology in general, particular knowledge is assumed to be inscrutable, and thus this information may come to dominate its creators. A kind of metalanguage, as Marcuse argues, "abstracts from the immediate concreteness in order to attain true concreteness."[19] Consequently, the opinions of those experts who have access to this technology, and thus objectivity, tend to be accepted with few reservations. Whereas previously a consultation with a variety practitioners may have been requested to verify a diagnosis, a computer can supply what the public has been led to believe is an infallible judgement. Undoubtedly, computer-based diagnosis can become easily cloaked in mystery.

To paraphrase Szasz, the manufacture of madness can reach new levels as a consequence of computerization.[20] The stage can be set where the inferiorization of clients is commonplace, because their frame of reference and cognitive processes can never be as reliable as the knowledge base of a computer. Therefore, almost by definition, a computerized diagnostic scheme comes to epitomize rationality, while lesser forms of classification and examination are discredited as replete with emotion and judged to be biased. In more concrete terms, clients are presumed to be subjective, while clinicians are objective. When this asymmetry is tolerated, clients are not in a position to be self-directing.

In a manner of speaking, a technological straitjacket may be imposed on clients as a result of computerizing social services. Due to the exaggerated claims that are often accepted about technological rationality, other styles of reasoning may be dismissed as lacking credibility. To be given credence, a client's views must conform to the standards for valid knowledge that are associated with computerization. Clinicians are thus in a position to manipulate patients in the name of scientific inquiry. After all, clients who are distressed and seeking treatment may not likely question a clinician who has evidence derived from a computer. Further, they may even be identified as defying reason. Hence, manipulation may result from adhering to standardized practices, which appear to be very credible. Precisely because the diagnostic process appears to be impersonal, questions may not be raised pertaining to the clinical judgments that are rendered.

Due to the complicated nature of technology and the shroud of objectivity that surrounds the use of computers, clients may be consigned to playing a secondary role in therapy. Clinical judgments that are generated by a computer appear to be scientific, and thus may be given undue respect. At the same time, the input of clients may be downgraded in importance, thereby providing practitioners with almost unlimited latitude to dictate a treatment regimen. Hence, therapy may become, at minimum, a subtle form of manipulation.

## Testing vs. Evaluation

At one time, treatment was not individualized. General labels were used to identify classes of patients. Also, standard treatments were prescribed for each malady. In short, making diagnoses and providing treatment were routine activities which did not necessarily take into account a client's biography, cultural orientation, or value base. Intervention was mechanistic, the general outcome being that patients were treated inconsiderately. And due to this insensitivity, very little insight was gained into the social side of mental illness. Expedient classification was the norm, while the experience of madness was ignored. But contrary to this viewpoint,

Loren Mosher and Lorenzo Burti argue correctly that "community mental health is psychosocial."[21]

According to some modern writers, patients have been obscured by technical protocol.[22] Armed with a plethora of tests, drugs, and other clinical paraphernalia, clinicians have proceeded to classify and mistreat patients without much resistance. What clients were actually experiencing or saying was interpreted according to psychiatric nomenclature, and thus the interpretive, or human, factor was buried under a host of clinical and administrative demands. As is suggested, the uniqueness of clients was overlooked, and they were, thus, dehumanized.

Since 1963, however, clients are guaranteed the right to individualized care. As part of this requirement, intervention is supposed to be sensitive to a community's values and comprehensible. For example, diagnoses should be made based on the rules that determine community competence, as opposed to abstract clinical criteria. This means that a community's standards of decorum should serve to differentiate health from illness. Furthermore, intervention that violates the sensibilities of a community can be refused without reprisal. In short, treatment is comprehensible when it is consistent with a community's world-view.

Yet practitioners should be aware that the appearance of computers may result in tempering these requirements. Specifically, evaluation can easily become synonymous with testing. Due to the push to computerize every aspect of service delivery, mechanized test administration, scoring, and interpreting can become increasingly enticing. Although conducting an evaluation should be much more extensive than administering a battery of tests, this strategy may be encouraged because the use of computerized clinical instruments saves time and money. And in this period of retrenchment, logistical considerations such as these have become paramount to many program managers.

Emphasizing efficiency in this way, however, has several dire consequences. First, so-called quick and dirty evaluations may become commonplace, when information that cannot or has not been prepared for computerization may be excluded regularly from assessments. Hence, evaluations may become very superficial. Second, test selection may begin to be made in terms of technical criteria, rather than more sound clinical reasons. In other words, tests that have been computerized may be utilized more often than those that have not. Third, persons who do not have clinical training may come to monopolize the process of evaluation. In point of fact, companies that will administer, score, and interpret tests for a wide range of agencies have begun to proliferate. For a nominal fee, experienced clinicians may eventually be replaced by computer technicians. Finally, automated testing may begin to appear in various nonclinical settings. Due to the availability of computerized tests, police or school officials may decide to launch mandatory testing programs. The damage that may result from such policies could be devastating.

In sum, automated evaluations may deprive clients of their right to socially sensitive treatment. Formalized evaluations that are undertaken by computer technicians are anathema to this need. But once efficiency begins to guide the evaluation process, raising nontechnical questions begins to be viewed as a luxury. Nonetheless, individualized interventions are not efficient, because standardized responses are disallowed. Whereas the thrust of technical reason is economy, care that is socially sensitive is multidimensional. Evaluations, therefore, should include a diverse number of assessment strategies. A requirement of socially sensitive treatment is that assessments extend beyond practices usually defined as technically efficient.

Individualized treatment plans and goal attainment scaling were proposed, for example, so that therapy could be personalized.[23] These modes of evaluation can be computerized, without necessarily negating the principle of multidimensionality that is key to community based intervention. However, the prevailing notion of efficiency must be redefined. Restricting the scope of evaluations may at first appear to be rational, until inaccurate assessments result in misdiagnoses and increased recidivism. Yet when technical factors are of paramount importance, social costs are given minimum attention. Technical reasoning, therefore, should not be allowed to blind practitioners to the contextual elements that are essential to an adequate definition of efficiency. It must be remembered that efficiency is not simply an economic construct. Personal and collective goals are related to a meaningful rendition of efficiency.

## Patient Confidentiality

Clients must be insured that their records and conversations with therapists will remain confidential. According to Levy, "the sharing of secrets and confidences . . . and the assurance that they will remain confidential are necessary for the very performance of . . . service."[24] Actually, a wide range of issues are covered under what at first may appear to be a simple mandate. In general, practitioners should recognize that persons are still stigmatized for reporting to treatment. Even though the theory of mental illness and service delivery has changed, much of the public and clinical-medical establishment continue to believe that this problem stems from biological causes, moral weakness, or some combination of these factors.[25] In order to preserve the integrity of society, the unfortunate individuals who manifest symptoms of mental illness are identified and, in many ways, kept from associating freely with the remainder of the world. While most patients today are not locked away in a state hospital, emotional barriers prevent them from being integrated into society.

The problem with this reaction is that persons delay seeking treatment until the last possible moment. Of course, delay often results in damage to other institutions, such as the family, that are not equipped to deal with a member who exhibits bizarre behavior. Causing this disruption, furthermore, only proves to the public that these persons should not be trusted. Yet once treatment is entered, stigmatization often continues, according to Goffman, as clients begin their "moral careers."[26] Often patients are not allowed direct access to their charts, information that is revealed in private conversations is given regularly to researchers and other third parties, and client records typically circulate freely among persons who are merely tangentially involved in the treatment process. The point is that any errors in clinical judgment are supposed to favor the public; the public demands the right to be protected from those who defy reason. Although mental illness is supposed to represent problems in living, rather than a by-product of diabolical forces, the public remains convinced that this is not the case.

Because of the adversarial relationship between patients and the public, those who desire treatment must be protected until the proper education occurs that will reduce this conflict. Unless confidentiality can be promised, even the limited number of persons enrolled in treatment will likely decline. Additionally, clinical rapport will probably not improve. "It is commonly believed," claims Reamer, "that if a meaningful, therapeutic relationship is to develop, a client must be able to assume that information shared with a social worker will be kept confidential."[27] Yet how may the introduction of computers into this hostile environment further undermine the possibility that a client will not be harmed by an inquiring, but uninformed, public?

Most difficult to address, as suggested by Burnham, is that in the Computer Age all knowledge appears to be public.[28] Knowledge is simply a resource that resides in large reservoirs that can be entered by anyone who has the proper equipment. Once information is placed in a data bank, for example, the personal character of this knowledge is diminished. Many new laws and educational strategies will have to be developed to reinforce the idea that no information is inherently public property. What is considered to be within the public domain should be a result of discussion and agreement, rather than a matter of where information is stored or the type of knowledge involved. The neutralization of knowledge attendant to computerization should not be allowed to rob knowledge of its personality. Clients should never be viewed as merely "data persons" who are abstract and cannot be hurt by indiscretions.[29]

On a less philosophical note, the guarantee of privileged communication may be jeopardized. In fact, data banks are not necessarily secure and can be infiltrated unless elaborate precautions are taken.[30] New York state, for example, has become a leader in this area. Complicated policies and procedures have been instituted, in addition to a network of safety codes, to limit access to the state's computerized file system. As might be suspected, much time and effort went into this undertaking. However, due to decreases in funding, this sort of planning may become too costly and security may be compromised. Protecting clients from unwanted intrusions may become exceedingly complex and prohibitive in terms of administrative priorities. But a brief lapse of vigilance concerning large data banks can culminate in a massive breach of confidentiality.

On the personal level several difficulties may arise. New problems related to the release of information may be encountered. The number of information requests may proliferate, due to the perceived ease of accessibility. Thus, sheltering clients may require increasingly sophisticated and expensive schemes. When conducting research investigators will have to be very careful, because information requests made to many data banks are recorded on tape. Unbeknownst to many researchers, these recordings can often be reviewed by anyone. Yet giving researchers immediate access to data may provide them with unauthorized admission to the records of clients who are not being studied. And finally, direct access of clients to their records may be thwarted. But if clients are able to learn the computer system, another security risk is posed.

Computerized record keeping may initially save an organization money. However, preserving the security of these systems may eventually become very costly. Anticipating and counteracting every possible security threat can become unbelievably time consuming. Additionally, the resulting data banks can be extremely cumbersome and thus unmanageable. In short, insuring the confidentiality of information contained in an automated file can quickly appear to reach a point of diminishing returns.

### Informed Consent

Nowadays clients must understand and consent to all the treatments that are tried. But in the not so distant past persons could be signed into treatment by a relative, and have little or no legal recourse to reverse this course of action. And as is illustrated in practically every psychology textbook, patients were subjected to all sorts of hideous practices against their will.[31] For example, experimental drugs were administered without any understanding of their effects. Moreover, in order to control patients, they were often physically mutilated and left in a semi-conscious state, thereby making custodial care easier.

Such manipulation is no longer acceptable. Richard Zaner rightly notes that patients should have "accurate, adequate, and understandable information...promptly and continuously given to them."[32] Accordingly, the relationship that is engendered between clients and their therapists is supposed to be based on a contract. Implied is that these parties are supposed to be viewed as equals in the process whereby treatment plans are created. Clinicians should no longer act paternalistically toward clients, with regard to any facet of intervention. For example, the known and even the range of likely side effects of drugs must be explained to clients. Further, involvement in research and experimental projects is optional. In other words, clients must be fully informed about every step in their treatment. As should be noted, consent is very different from assent. And by signing their treatment plans, clients are given a formal opportunity to reject a course of action.

But what does informed consent mean in the age of computer use? Traditionally this idea has been invoked to protect clients from physical harm, although psychological harm is now also typically understood to be covered by this concept.[33] Yet the question remains, how much of computerized intervention does a client have to understand? Since patients may be involved *directly* with computers, how much information do they need about software and hardware? How much technical knowledge does a client have the right to demand? After all, becoming informed about high-tech treatment may require that clients receive extensive training. For example, how a client's responses are understood by a computer program may affect the choices he or she will make. Should a client be informed that when ELIZA responds "In what way?" it is merely a ploy to gain additional information? Do clients have the right to understand fully the intricacies of computerization?

In addition to understanding procedures, clients must be made aware of the likely consequences of a treatment. At this time, a paucity of research exists pertaining to the impact of computerized intervention.[34] And even the data that do exist are anything but clear. Are minority or elderly clients affected adversely by assessments that are computerized? Questions such as these need to be addressed before informed consent can be given by a patient. Why should a person be discriminated against by the mere nature of a procedure?

Clearly, new areas of concern have been opened relative to informed consent as a result of the introduction of computers into the therapeutic setting. After all, computer-based judgments are made in terms of knowledge that is not widely disseminated. And dealing with machines, rather than human beings, in the therapeutic setting, certainly stretches the bounds of informed consent. Even the assumptions on which clients and therapists act are called into question, due to the possible cultural impact of the computer microworld. Practitioners should begin to recognize that being informed nowadays is not as straightforward as in earlier days. But Elliot Friedson makes a crucial point that should not be forgotten: "Depersonalization is most marked when the client is most helpless, when the choice and arrangement of services is an exclusive prerogative of management."[35]

## TREATMENT AND SURVEILLANCE

Personal privacy is considered to be essential for successful treatment. "For privacy is the necessary context for relationships which we would hardly be human if we had to do without—the relationships of love, friendship and trust."[36] Minimally, this means that a facility should not be overcrowded. The large and impersonal wards that were used in the past are now believed to be degrading and not conducive to therapy. Space must be available where clients can express themselves freely. Furthermore, how can treatment occur if so many patients are present that only infrequent and perfunctory contact between these persons and their therapist is possible? In other words, the basic structure of a treatment facility should be therapeutic.

Clients should feel safe, live in comfortable surroundings, and have the opportunity to privately discuss issues related to treatment. Yet insuring privacy extends beyond environmental concerns. Uniqueness of style, personal expression, freedom of thought and demeanor, and autonomy should all be encouraged. A sense of physical and psychological (existential) space should be protected.

These personal areas may shrink dramatically as a consequence of computerization. As a result of creating what Lyon calls a "Panopticon of fibre optics and remote terminals," a client's personal space can be easily invaded.[37] Already available are techniques that allow clients to be monitored every minute of the day, both inside and outside of a treatment facility. However, this is not all. Physiological measurements have been developed that can probe inner space, in order to determine whether someone is telling the truth. Further, due to the presence of large and interconnected data banks, background checks that are more extensive than ever before imagined can be regularly undertaken. Through the use of computer technology even the innermost dimensions of a person's life can be violated.

Typically the privacy question is limited to physical space. With the advent of computerized monitoring, however, psychic, emotional, and interpersonal space are no longer sacred. The type of social control that is possible through the use of computers is phenomenal. In this regard, treatment facilities can begin to resemble the Panopticon discussed by Michel Foucault.[38] As is suggested by this term, the vision of practitioners can extend to the soul of those who are watched. Nothing is sacred; there is no place where a patient can retreat alone.

Given the ubiquity of monitoring, how can therapy be expected to occur? The situation Foucault describes is far worse than that found in the grim institutions described by Goffman.[39] Goffman could never have envisioned the control capabilities that would accompany recent technological developments. With control extending to the core of a person's existence, rebellion or even raising questions is not very likely. The prospects for treatment, however, are also not very favorable. As mentioned earlier, therapy and constraint are no longer thought to be synonymous. Instead, clients must be able to exhibit the initiative necessary to make choices and resolve problems. Enough freedom must be granted so that they can master the skills vital to independent living. Surely the existential confinement that is possible due to technological rationality is anathema to fostering a therapeutic environment that is client-centered. A technological straitjacket may be unobtrusive, yet clients are still constrained.

Because of the power of technical reason to establish an almost impermeable web of psychic and physical restraints, new guidelines must be proposed with respect to monitoring clients. Evaluations must not be permitted to become surveillance. Restrictions must be placed on how many tests are to be conducted, when and where monitoring devices can be used, and the amount and types of information that can be included in a background check. Now that practically every aspect of a client's life can be monitored, the possibility of degradation is greater than ever before. Therefore, special care must be taken to insure that the surveillance capability of computers is not abused.

## CONCLUSION

Dealing with ethical considerations within the technical ethos that has come to dominate modern society is very difficult. In short, human issues tend to be resolved in technical terms; a concern for proper calculation replaces the desire to ascertain whether an act is good or bad. Yet the question of whether a plan of action should be undertaken is unrelated to technology. When and how technology is utilized depends on more fundamental issues. In this case, values pertaining to the importance of human dignity establish the parameters for service delivery. Specifically, a humanly inspired code of ethics is supposed to guarantee that "therapists will demonstrate a sensible regard for the social mores and expectations of the community."[40] Nonetheless, there is a strong temptation to translate ethical themes into technical ones, due to the lure of technological rationality.

The emphasis currently placed on high-tech instruments should not blind practitioners to the perennial ethical concerns of philosophers, which have kept society somewhat humane. Just because a client can be observed twenty-four hours a day, should this kind of surveillance be tolerated? Answering this question depends on the image of society a group of persons hold dear. And since 1963, this kind of mortification—involving a loss of autonomy, self-determination, and freedom of action—is deemed unacceptable.[41] Technology should not be allowed to undermine this progressive stance, but should be merely one of many variables given attention during a client's treatment. As a result, the choices that guide intervention should never be compromised by technical developments.

Due to the expediency encouraged by technology, practitioners should not be lulled into a sense of laziness. Indeed, addressing ethical problems is rough. Progress has been made in the mental health care area that must not be sacrificed, because questions of an ethical nature tend to be disruptive. Whereas technical systems are neatly integrated and appear to be devoid of conflict, ethical systems never reach a state of closure. New possibilities always arise that must be settled. In fact, ethical questions may signal the need for social change. Moreover, the skills required to assess these issues critically must not be allowed to atrophy, or clients may be simply controlled in the most efficient manner ever envisioned. Such a step backward must be averted at all cost.

## NOTES

1. Andrew T. Scull, *Museums of Madness* (New York: St. Martin's Press, 1979).

2. J. K. Wing and G. W. Brown, *Institutionalism and Schizophrenia* (London: Cambridge University Press, 1970).

3. August B. Hollingshead and Frederick C. Redlich, *Social Class and Mental Illness* (New York: Wiley, 1958), pp. 171-229.

4. Erving Goffman, *Asylums* (Chicago: Aldine, 1961), pp. 1-124.

5. J. K. Wing, *Reasoning About Madness* (Oxford: Oxford University Press, 1978), pp. 26-27.

6. Robert Sommer, "Patients Who Grow in a Mental Hospital," *Geriatrics* 14(6) (1959): pp. 586-587.

7. John F. Kennedy, "Mental Illness and Mental Retardation—Message from the President," *Congressional Record* (Washington, DC: Government Printing Office, 1963), pp. 1837-1842.

8. *Implementing Standards to Assure the Rights of Mental Patients* (Washington, DC: Department of Health and Human Services, 1980).

9. Loren R. Mosher and Lorenzo Burti, *Community Mental Health* (New York: W. W. Norton, 1989), p. 106.

10. Ivan Illich, *Medical Nemesis*, (New York: Bantam Books, 1976), pp. 47-130.

11. Szasz, *Ideology and Insanity*, pp. 12-24.

12. Pete Sedqwick, *Psycho-Politics* (New York: Harper and Row, 1982), pp. 3-42.

13. Benjamin Kleinmuntz, "The Scientific Study of Clinical Judgments in Psychology and Medicine," *Clinical Psychology Review* 4(2) (1984): pp. 111-126.

14. Dery, *Computers in Welfare*, p. 204.

15. Winner, *Autonomous Technology*, p. 257.

16. Charles S. Levy, *Social Work Ethics* (New York: Human Sciences Press, 1976), pp. 132-135.

17. David Held, *Introduction to Critical Theory* (Berkeley: University of California Press, 1980), pp. 263-267.

18. Marcuse, *One Dimensional Man*, p. 168.

19. Marcuse, *One Dimensional Man*, p. 180.

20. Thomas S. Szasz, *The Manufacture of Madness* (New York: Harper and Row, 1970).

21. Mosher and Burti, *Community Mental Health,* p. 47.

22. Derrida, *Writing and Difference,* pp. 31-63.

23. Thomas J. Kiresuk and Sander H. Lund, "Process and Outcome Measurement Using Goal Attainment Scaling," in *Program Evaluation: Alcohol, Drug Abuse, and Mental Health Services,* ed. Jack Zusman and Cecil R. Wurster (Lexington, MA: D.C. Heath, 1975), pp. 213-228.

24. Levy, *Social Work Ethics,* p. 51.

25. Ivan Illich, *Limits to Medicine* (New York: Penguin Books, 1977), pp. 47-130.

26. Goffman, *Asylums,* pp. 3-12.

27. Frederic G. Reamer, *Ethical Dilemmas in Social Service* (New York: Columbia University Press, 1982), p. 120.

28. David Burnham, *The Rise of the Computer State* (New York: Random House, 1983).

29. Lyon, *The Information Society,* p. 103.

30. John M. Carroll, *Computer Security,* 2nd ed. (Boston: Butterworths, 1987).

31. Longmire and Callahan, "The Role of Reason in the Social Control of Mental Illness," pp. 53-65.

32. Richard M. Zaner, "How the Hell Did I Get Here," in *Caring, Curing, and Coping: Nurse, Physician, and Patient Relationships,* ed. A. N. Bishop and John R. Scudder (Birmingham: University of Alabama Press, 1985), p. 95.

33. Lawrence Tancredi, "The New Technology of Psychiatry: Ethics, Epidemiology, and Technology Assessment," in *Ethical Issues in Epidemiologic Research,* ed. Lawrence Tancredi (New Brunswick, NJ: Rutgers University Press, 1986), pp. 1-36.

34. Jonathan D. Leiff, *Computer Applications in Psychiatry* (Washington, DC: American Psychiatric Press, 1987), pp. 135-248.

35. Elliot Friedson, "Health Factories, the New Industrial Sociology," in *Freedom and Tyranny,* ed. Jack D. Douglas (New York: Knopf, 1970), p. 217.

36. Charles Fried, "Privacy [A Moral Analysis]," in *Philosophical Dimensions of Privacy,* ed. Ferdinand David Schoeman (Cambridge: Cambridge University Press, 1984), p. 211.

37. Lyon, *The Information Society,* p. 99.

38. Michel Foucault, *Discipline and Punish* (New York: Pantheon Books, 1977), p. 99.

39. Goffmen, *Asylums,* pp. 173-320.

40. William H. Van Hoos and Jeffrey A. Kottler, *Ethical and Legal Issues in Counseling and Psychotherapy* (San Francisco: Jossey-Bass, 1980), p. 7.

41. Goffman, *Asylums,* p. 43.

# 9

---

# Creating a Socially
# Responsible Technology

## INTRODUCTION

Throughout this book the point has been made that at the basis of computerization is dualism.[1] As a consequence of this particular theoretical maneuver, the illusion is created that the use of computers is value-free. Hence, data can be identified, classified, and processed with minimal interruption.

But this refinement has a high cost. Completely externalizing the production of knowledge, in other words, may have deleterious social consequences. Computerization can easily culminate in alienation, when the generation and application of information is reified. If the strictures imposed to gather data begin to dictate the identity and utility of input, practitioners are no longer in control of service delivery. From the standpoint of the technological ethic, notes Ellul, this discovery is not all bad.[2] Because, according to the principles of dualism, human involvement in any activity introduces unnecessary error and uncertainty.

Given the hegemony of technique, human values, interpretations, and judgments are diminished in importance. In fact, these considerations are thought to impede making service delivery scientific. The lure of becoming scientific, combined with the almost magical character of computer technology, places practitioners in a difficult position. Those who question the worth of computers, and try to temper their impact, are often criticized and dismissed as Luddites. And those who unquestioningly accept computers are cajoled inadvertently into ignoring the possible dehumanizing effects of these instruments. Either way, the rights of clients may not be protected.

What is needed, therefore, is a new approach to computerization. An awareness must be promoted that those who view the widespread computerization of human services as dubious are not necessarily ignorant or trying to inhibit progress. Likewise, the understanding should be promoted that computers may be used in a socially sensitive manner, without automatically transforming intervention into a "touchy-feely" endeavor. Stated differently, the effectiveness of practitioners should not necessarily be suspect simply because they question the worth of computers or suggest that these devices may have utility. What about the idea that computers can be used in a socially responsible manner?

This statement is not intended to resurrect the tired notion that computers should be designed to fulfill human aims. Although this sentiment is nice, merely wishing for improvements is insufficient to make computer use humane. Due to the effects of dualism, computers are not readily amenable to this shift in orientation. If this technology has begun to dominate service delivery, and thus is intrusive and unresponsive, claiming that computers are really tools and potentially useful will not solve these problems. A much more sophisticated response is needed.

Instead, the perpetrator of this technological slavery must be challenged. The factor that creates the "technology is autonomous" charade must be exposed and illustrated to be an inappropriate base for computer use. What this means is that dualism must be undermined and replaced by a more embodied rationale for substantiating computerization. Computerization, in other words, must not be allowed to obscure the human element. The computer microworld must not be permitted to undermine the volition that originally gave rise to this mode of conceptualization.

Ortega y Gasset remarked once that the human element will be expanding long after the potential of technology has been exhausted.[3] His point is that technology represents a modality of human experience, but somehow this understanding has been lost.

Transforming the use of computers so that this technology does not violate everyday affairs will not be easy, because this maneuver requires antidualistic thinking that is not commonplace. At both the theoretical and practical levels dualism must undermined.

Through a variety of tactics, the apparent autonomy of technical reason must be subverted. In this way, an essential connection between this form of rationality and human action can be reestablished. Computer technology can thus truly be placed in the service of humanity. Technological rationality will lose its seignorial status, along with those who have privileged access to this knowledge. What this means is that computer-based information will have limited utility, which is based on a host of factors including values, beliefs, aspirations, and social or cultural context. Like other styles of knowledge, the insights provided by computerization will no longer be viewed as ahistorical.

Consistent with Gadamer's definition of ahistorical, this term does not simply mean that computers will be understood to originate from a particular location or period.[4] Much more important, the aim is to show that computerization is a human invention, finite, and equal to other methods of reasoning. As a result, the utility of computer technology cannot be assumed to originate from technical advances, but from value judgments; only certain commitments can elevate technical reason over other forms of reason. Clearly, viewing computerization in this way relativizes computer-based knowledge, thereby reducing the likelihood of technological slavery.

## REFLEXIVE ENVIRONMENT

What needs to be done, therefore, is to place computerization in a reflexive environment.[5] The idea at this juncture is that a framework can be generated whereby the limitations of technical rationality can be easily recognized. Computers can be placed in a philosophical, organizational, or managerial context that is not dualistic, so that the possible antagonism between this technology and humans is reduced. Therefore, this mode of technological rationality can be supplemented by other kinds of knowledge and values, without the fear that validity and reliability will be sacrificed. All that occurs, instead, is that computerization can no longer be automatically cited as the paragon of rationality.

The concept of reflexivity is not new. Alvin Gouldner popularized the use of this term in the early 1970s, with his call for a "reflexive sociology."[6] Nowadays Niklas Luhmann has adapted this theme to institutional analysis.[7] Luhmann asks if reflexivity can be built into social institutions in order to make these organizations more responsible to the desires of citizens. What both of these critics have in mind is to foster the general democratization of society. Obviously such a proposal has relevance for computer use. For if computerization and the application of this process could be democratized, many of the problems attendant to the implementation of computer technology could be averted.

How can reflexivity rehabilitate technology? Associated with this concept are several key ideas that provide computer use with a human ground. Most significant, as might be expected, dualism is demonstrated to be outmoded.

Due to reflexivity, the awareness is promoted that no form of knowledge is autonomous. As Gouldner notes, revealed by a reflexive sociology are the "domain assumptions" that "entail beliefs about what is real in the world."[8] His point is that fact and value cannot be clearly differentiated; beliefs cannot be separated neatly from reality. If this schism were feasible, facts would be pristine or disconnected from interpretation. Advocates of reflexivity, however, contend that this is never the case. Knowledge always exists *in situ* and is affected by definitions, the methodologies employed to gather data, and situational contingencies. Walter Benjamin captured the thrust of this component of reflexivity when he recognized that perception is always simultaneously interpretation. As a result, he writes that "there is no event or thing either animate or inanimate that does not in some way participate in language."[9]

Postmodernists write that once knowledge, even that associated with computerization, is connected intimately with interpretation, the standard separation between appearances and reality becomes increasingly difficult to justify. The reason for this is quite simple: reality is not ultimately real but is implicated in certain assumptions that distinguish fact from fantasy. According to Lyotard, "there wouldn't be any space or time independent of a phrase."[10] Following the acceptance of particular assumptions about phenomena such as space, time, motion, and so forth, reality begins to emerge. In short, reality is not a spectacle, but is embedded within a particular conceptual scheme.

Hence, reality and assumptions that are existentially mediated are inextricably united. And shifts in these assumptions result in changes in the nature of reality. But once reality is understood to be the product of presuppositions, generalizations can be made only with many qualifications. After all, assumptions cannot be extended indefinitely. For their relevance is, almost by definition, well circumscribed. In the case of computer technology, this means that the logic, conceptual apparatus, and theoretical justification for computerization do not have inherent legitimacy. Recognition of these ideas is gained through a social process that is usually viewed as ancillary to computerization.

A reflexive person is not enamored of reality, because facts cannot be removed from the assumptions that are made about knowledge. Furthermore, these beliefs must be given credence before they gain ascendancy over others. The melange of competing assumptions, in other words, is calmed only through human intervention. Reality is thus understood to depend on volition, rather than traits that have unflagging validity. This means that computer-based knowledge must compete with other styles of information, if computerization is to be viewed as valuable. Introducing computers into such an environment will help to prevent this technology from gaining the autonomy that can be very harmful.

Yet how can reflexivity be brought to fruition? For merely ruminating about this activity will not make it viable. What is required, instead, is a policy that contains vital philosophical and organizational components. As part of humanizing agencies, perhaps postmodernism can be of assistance in this endeavor? As a result of the comprehensive planning encouraged by postmodernists, reflexivity has a reasonable chance of succeeding.

## PHILOSOPHY AND DUALISM

Postmodernism has become quite vogue in a variety of disciplines, due to its antidualistic orientation.[11] Most radical about this position is the proclamation that the traditional internal/external bifurcation is not valid. The unadulterated knowledge sought by proponents of Cartesianism, in other words, is considered to be passé. As a direct challenge to dualism, knowledge is considered to have a human or fleshy texture. As Merleau-Ponty writes, "my body is made of the same flesh as the world . . . and moreover . . . this flesh of my body is shared by the world."[12] As is suggested by Merleau-Ponty's statement, postmodernists insist that facts cannot be extricated from the body.

What is the intent of this kind of argument? Remember that Descartes categorically separated the mind and body, for he believed that allowing them to intermingle would be disastrous. Truth would be lost forever, because the body is the source of desire and opinion, and thus error. In order to safeguard facts, dualists such as Descartes attempt to supply knowledge with a foundation that is supposed to be unaffected by interpretation.

But postmodernists charge this demarcation is a chimera, because all knowledge is mediated completely by language, even the data procured through positive science.[13] Language is not a surrogate for a more profound reality, but rather pervades everything that is known. Stepping outside of language is thus impossible. Using the idiom of formal logic, for them p does not equal q but, instead, p almost equals q. "P and -p," writes Lyotard, are merely "limited cases."[14]

What is the importance of this maneuver for computerization? Clearly challenged is the binary logic that makes computer use possible, characterized by the proposition $A = A$. Conveyed by this notation is a variant of essentialism that suggests facts, events, or persons have a fundamental identity.[15] Therefore, categorizing these and other phenomena is considered to be a logistical issue that can be addressed through a technical means.

When speech acts are ubiquitous to knowledge, however, securing the identity of A becomes problematic. At any time the meaning of A can change, thereby suggesting that A may be equal to B, C, D, and so on. As is the case with dialectical logic, the interpenetration of opposites becomes a dominant theme. Identities are thus elusive and are not readily transformed into technical protocol. Additionally, the meaning of input can be captured, advise postmodernists, only by consulting the language game operative in a specific location.

Yet the aim of computerization is to formalize data processing, rather than introduce a host of contingencies. If every piece of information must be qualified, nothing is gained by using a computer. Nonetheless, the influence of interpretation will not simply vanish. This means that many of the theoretical tenets that sustain computerization must be reassessed.

For example, due to the pervasiveness of interpretation, computer space is not pure but a social invention. Suggested by this claim is that this is not a sanitary realm where classification can proceed with little regard for existential concerns. In fact, postmodernists write that knowledge must be regionalized rather than universalized, due to the way language use shifts affect the nature of truth. Lyotard makes this point by quoting René Thom: "The more or less determined character of a process is determined by the local state of the process."[16] In other words, the identity of knowledge cannot be separated from the search for truth. The illusion is difficult to maintain, therefore, that data processing is value-free and undoubtedly reliable. Reality assumptions are not eliminated by computerization, but, at best, are concealed in a sophisticated manner. Even within the sphere deployed by computer space, the influence of language is never thoroughly suppressed. Computerization is thus always value-based.

This philosophical move has interesting consequences for computerization. Most important is that attention is focused on the impact of the computer microworld. Accordingly, computer-based decisions are illustrated to be made within a realm replete with epistemological values, along with political and other social implications. Computerizing a diagnosis, for example, does not necessarily neutralize the clinical protocol that are used. All that occurs is these criteria are obscured behind a facade of objectivity, thereby diverting criticism to technical issues. Yet classifying persons and correcting their behavior is a political act, even when accomplished via the computer.

Does giving computer space a linguistic base necessarily result in the demise of computerization? The obvious answer is no. But the application of computer technology is certainly placed under close scrutiny. For even when they are adopted to perform the most mundane tasks, computers are recognized to be shaping input. Perhaps when collecting demographic information on clients this influence will be minimal. And with regard to certain types of behavioral therapy, distorting how clients perceive reality is assumed to be inconsequential. However, when computers are employed to actually engage clients in therapeutic dialogue, overlooking the need for interpersonal sensitivity will undoubtedly have deleterious consequences.

The point is that attacking dualism philosophically places computerization in a new light. The autonomy of computer space is exposed to be illusory, while attention is directed to understanding the ways in which information can be reified through computerization. In short, the alleged innocence of computers is challenged; their potential ideological character is exposed.

## EPISTEMOLOGICAL PLURALISM

An undesirable consequence of computerization is the monopolization of knowledge. In other words, a particular kind of knowledge and/or select persons may begin to dominate the intervention process. Due to the alleged objective nature of computer-based data, all other information is often treated as inadequate. Moreover, those who have access to knowledge that is generated through computers are accorded special status in agencies. A case in point is provided by those who administer, score, and interpret tests. Often these persons are not trained except in the operation of computers, but their judgments are nonetheless regularly the centerpiece of a client's treatment plan.

This gradual professionalization of services is especially problematic at this time. In violation of the spirit and letter of the Community Mental Health Act, clients are moved to the periphery of the planning process. Because their input is not viewed as objective or scientific, their insights are often discounted. Stanley Cohen remarks that this "centralization" of valuable knowledge constitutes an unobtrusive, yet extremely effective, means of social control.[17] The criticisms voiced by clients can be easily discredited by scientists, thereby enhancing the power of those who administer agencies. Although the total institutions described by Goffman may be disappearing, human service agencies may still enforce social control.[18] Only now restraint is enacted through seemingly apolitical means. After all, do inanimate objects such as computers have political ambitions?

How can this undesirable side effect of computerization be avoided? Another step toward creating a humane technology relates to fostering epistemological pluralism. The aim is to reduce the likelihood that other than computer-based knowledge will be treated as worthless. Therefore, the awareness must be promoted that restricting the growth of knowledge is both inefficient and ineffective. Economy in the use of information, in other words, is unproductive.

The centralization of knowledge is predicated on a dubious principle. That is, certain data are objective, or accepted as objective, while other information is believed to be inherently contaminated by opinion. Furthermore, the more removed knowledge is from this unadulterated center, the less valuable this information becomes.

But postmodernists declare that the world should be understood as "centerless."[19] What they mean is that a reality *sui generis* cannot be invoked to serve as an absolute measure of valid knowledge. Instead of being hierarchically arranged around an absolute referent, knowledge is organized in a patchwork. Especially in view of Thom's Catastrophe Theory, postmodernists maintain that knowledge should be viewed as constrained by the element of interpretation.[20]

Once dualism is rejected, as suggested earlier in this chapter, all knowledge is placed on an identical plane. Because every sort of input is replete with assumptions, no knowledge automatically supplies a complete picture of a problem. And thus no knowledge base should be allowed to inferiorize other alternatives. Each source of input merely fills in another part of the mosaic. Rather than the cornerstone of a diagnosis, for example, a computer-based test provides merely one perspective on a problem. Similarly, the insights of clients are not consigned to supplementing other, more scientific findings.

In this sense the intervention process is democratized. What Guattari refers to as the "despotism of the signifier" is undermined.[21] To be effective, therefore, a practitioner should consult as many sources of knowledge as possible. In fact, failing to do so results in inefficiency that cannot be rectified by introducing the bias present in positive science. Because knowledge has limited parameters, effort must be exerted to join apparently disparate views. For the integrity of every viewpoint must be protected if an accurate assessment of an issue is to occur. Information should not be ignored simply because it originates from particular persons or is unrelated to scientific or technical protocol, for efficiency results from open competition among ideas. This kind of pluralism will not survive, however, unless the appropriate epistemological conditions are established.

## THE METAPHYSICS OF INTEGRATION

Pluralism requires a new and progressive imagery. In other words, an appropriate metaphysics of integration is needed.[22] A conceptual scheme must be proposed that allows divergent types of knowledge to be integrated, without a hint of reductionism. Unless this revolutionary imagery is forthcoming, data will likely be juxtaposed but not integrated. A pertinent example is provided by the current significance placed on holism by many practitioners. Although many options may be tolerated, these choices are often assigned a value *a priori*. Rigid strictures are thus imposed on the use of knowledge. In point of fact, even when holism is stressed, knowledge bases are usually arranged asymmetrically.

To correct this situation, systems theory has become vogue.[23] Clearly the strength of this philosophy is its comprehensiveness. No phenomenon is supposed to be understood to exist in isolation; various types of knowledge or events are thought to be interdependent. As a result of this awareness, the vision of practitioners is supposed to be enlarged. Instead of focusing primarily on psychological factors, for example, environmental considerations are supposed to be introduced into a diagnosis. In this way, holism is enacted.

Conceptualizing the relationship between knowledge bases in this manner will help temper the impact of computerization. However, using systems theory will not necessarily accomplish this aim. The reason for this unfavorable conclusion is quite simple: systems theory, as an outgrowth of cybernetics, is compatible with the incipient realism of computerization. As a consequence, the symmetrical integration of knowledge bases will not likely occur.

The key axiom of systems theory is that the whole is greater than the sum of the parts of any phenomenon.[24] Although at first this statement may appear innocuous, this is not the case. Inadvertently the stage is set for a particular viewpoint to be treated as transcending the system and assumed to be universal. Indeed, the parts of the system appear to be ancillary to a more fundamental framework. While this may not have been the intention of systems theorists, many practitioners seem to imagine the whole to be a preconceived and rigid system.

A prominent example is provided by the application of systems theory to family therapy.[25] While the initial purpose was to move away from psychological analysis and focus on the family as a functioning unit, increased insight was not necessarily a result of this maneuver. In short, the family was envisioned to consist of fixed roles designed to insure the survival of this institution. The members' actual behavior is thus interpreted regularly in terms of role requirements and seldom correctly understood.

Obviously, if computerization were to be treated in this way, the results would not be very favorable. The exalted status of computer-based knowledge would not necessarily be challenged, and thereby only pseudointegration would be possible. As long as the option is left for a particular knowledge base to be elevated over others, why should symmetrical integration be taken seriously?

For this reason, Gilles Deleuze and Felix Guattari,[26] along with Jean Gebser,[27] have introduced novel imagery to propagate epistemological pluralism. Deleuze and Guattari claim that the rhizome provides a perfect model for integrating knowledge. Likewise, Gebser refuses to call anything a system, but instead uses the term systase. In each case, these writers are arguing that reductionism will be averted only when knowledge is directly integrated, without the assistance of abstract props. A rhizome is neatly organized, yet the center of this plant is not obtrusive. "There are no points or positions on a rhizome...there are only lines," write Deleuze and Guattari.[28] Each part is integrated without the guidance provided by readily visible structures or abstract mechanisms.

What these newer, postmodern writers demonstrate is that the direct integration of knowledge is possible without chaos. Competition among knowledge bases does not have to culminate in either anarchy or one option eventually coming to overshadow all others. When order is conceived to be a systase or rhizome a more productive outcome is possible. Due to the absence of an absolute reality in each case, winning and losing is based on knowledge becoming thematic in particular contexts. The status of options can change, but only relative to each other. Accordingly, integration is maintained even when primacy is given temporarily to one knowledge base. Lyotard calls this a "tensor" relationship, which involves only divergences, differences, and comparisons, with no ultimate ground available to justify choices.[29] No matter what occurs, when knowledge bases are organized as a systase these various options are always complementary. As a result, preserving the integrity of each part is not antithetical to preserving integration.

## NONREPRESSIVE ORGANIZATIONS

In order to become epistemologically pluralistic, nondualistic organizations must be created. The conditions must be established so that input can be easily diversified. Through the implementation of nondualistic organizations, the autonomy of knowledge can be undermined as a result of promoting discussion and critique.

Yet at this time most social service agencies are bureaucracies. As described in chapter 3, due to the process of bureaucratization organizations begin to appear as if they are abstract. In other words, the organizational boundaries, information channels, and lines of authority are thoroughly rationalized and objectified. Hence, a vast amount of information can be processed with little effort, for extenuating circumstances are not allowed to influence decisions.

In the short run a bureaucracy seems to be efficient, for uniform pieces of information are classified according to standardized categories. But gradually efficiency begins to decline. Because of the stress that is placed on increased refinement and formalization, bureaucracies tend to become stodgy and unresponsive. Novel information that does not fit into the traditional plan is overlooked, while an inordinate amount of power begins to accrue to those who hold favored positions in an organization.

When computers are introduced into this scenario, input can become severely truncated. Access to computer-based information may become limited to a few experts, while the opinions of those who are not a part of this cabal are not often sought. Indeed, knowledge can rapidly become extremely centralized, without the proper type of organization to temper the impact of computers.

Initially, proponents of computerization thought this technology would foster the democratization of information use. This vision, however, proved to be false. Due to the indirect way bureaucracies are organized, with department linked at increasingly higher levels, fragmentation is practically unavoidable. Thus information is horded, communication is inaccurate and haphazard, and competition to create the most expansive and up-to-date data base is intense. With everyone acting on the basis of their own, and most technically advanced, source of information, organizations can easily become immobilized.

Those who are attempting to avoid this disaster are beginning to consider organizational correctives. Technical innovations alone are not thought to be sufficient to expand information flow, diversify input, and increase the sources of knowledge. Instead, computers must be situated in an organizational climate that is amenable to discussion and critique, so that the generation and implementation of information are not restricted by outmoded organizational imperatives.

As an alternative to bureaucracy, Likert's "linking-pin" style of organization has begun to receive some attention.[30] This is an example of the loosely coupled organization discussed earlier by Weick. According to Likert, the various segments of an organization can be directly linked. This is accomplished by assigning key persons from one department to participate in the planning of another unit. Organizational barriers are overcome, for the movement of both persons and information throughout an agency becomes normative. Because rigid boundaries are not imposed by Likert's model, flexibility is enhanced throughout an agency.

This is a nondualistic conception of the organization because roles are not based on structural imperatives. Rather, through discourse the goals, performance standards, and parameters of relevant data are established collectively. A case in point is provided by the creation of key report groups. These groups represent diverse segments of an organization and actually devise the criteria for identifying and utilizing relevant knowledge.[31] Input is not inhibited by strict organizational guidelines, but is solicited from throughout an agency. Professionals and nonprofessionals alike are given the opportunity to articulate their views.

When an organization is conceived in this way, introducing computers into an agency does not necessarily have to culminate in an extreme concentration of knowledge. Latitude is available for fostering discussion and raising criticisms, in addition to disseminating a broad range of information. Contributions are not based on rigidly conceived roles but are almost unlimited. The use of computer-based knowledge, in sum, may be dictated by the needs of clients, agency personnel, and citizens, instead of abstract organizational demands.

## PARTICIPATORY MANAGEMENT

Providing a permeable structure is insufficient to insure that an agency will become pluralistic. In addition to a flat organizational chart, an appropriate management philosophy must be adopted. To avoid the pitfalls of the bureaucrat trap, particularly defensiveness and resistance to new ideas, a participatory management style in necessary.[32] An essential ingredient to averting bureaucracy is a management philosophy that keeps an agency's structure open.

Both classical and more recent research indicates that a variety of benefits inure to a democratically managed organization.[33] In contrast to an authoritarian approach to management, morale and production are higher in democratically organized workplaces. Most relevant to the implementation of computer technology is that resistance to innovation is reduced by allowing employees to participate directly in the process of change. In this way, all personnel are able to become thoroughly familiar with computers and are not frightened by this technology.

What this shift in philosophy represents is the contention that centralized authority is ineffective. Many managers currently believe that those closest to a problem, have the requisite skills, and are most motivated should be included in decision making. Participation, in other words, should be as far reaching as is possible, so that many strategies and viewpoints can be tested when addressing an issue. When this policy is utilized workers will quickly support a novel project, thereby averting the pitfalls associated with piecemeal planning. Through the use of quality circles, quality of working life groups, and self-management, for example, employees throughout an agency can be provided with access to computer technology.

Due to this sort of participatory management, the mystique that typically surrounds computer technology can be unmasked. Those who are not experts no longer have to be intimidated by computers or computer-based knowledge. The subtle message conveyed by participatory management is that all employees, knowledge bases, and sources of input may add something significant to a discussion. Clearly this belief is crucial to the survival of pluralism and the democratization of knowledge use.


## CONCLUSION

This chapter introduced several themes that are vital to creating a reflexive environment. Most important is that through reflexivity, technological rationality is illustrated to be one of many modes of reason. Computers, accordingly, represented a limited means for generating knowledge. Computer-based knowledge simply embodies a specific discursive formation, as described by Foucault, which "is made up of a limited number of statements for which a group of conditions of existence can be defined."[34]

Computers are thus returned to what phenomenologists call the *Lebenswelt*, or life-world.[35] In simple terms, this means that computers are contextualized, which is just the opposite of what is intended by computerization. Correspondingly, the idea is promoted that an entire socialization process is involved in giving primacy to a particular knowledge base. Facts and objectivity are recognized to be socially constructed. Objectivity, stated differently, always reflects a perspective. Hence, applying computer-based knowledge is not fundamentally a technical issue. Instead, determining the proper application of computer-generated information is a social judgement.

In this chapter various theoretical and practical maneuvers that elevate in importance the social side of computer use were discussed. In each case, the distance between computer technology and the human element is reduced. With dualism discredited in this way, improving the human-technical interface, as opposed to merely adjusting users to the demands imposed by computerization, becomes a prerequisite for the rational use of computers.[36] Once dualism is revealed to be untenable, the belief in an autonomous technology will soon fade. Subsequently, the development of a humane technology will increasingly begin to make sense.

## NOTES

1. Lyotard, *The Postmodern Condition*, pp. 3-6.

2. Jacques Ellul, *The Technological Society* (New York: Vintage Books, 1964), p. 131.

3. José Ortega y Gasset, *History as a System* (New York: W.W. Norton, 1961), p. 13.

4. Gadamer, *Truth and Method*, p. 251.

5. John W. Murphy and John T. Pardeck, "The Development of 'Socially Responsible' Educational Technology," *Proceedings of the Fifth Annual Conference Applying New Technology in Higher Education*, (Manhattan, KS: Kansas State University, 1986), pp. 189-195.

6. Alvin Gouldner, *The Coming Crisis in Western Sociology* (New York: Basic Books, 1970), pp. 481-512.

7. Luhmann, *The Differentiation of Society*, pp. 324-362.

8. Gouldner, *The Coming Crisis in Western Sociology*, p. 48.

9. Walter Benjamin, *Reflections* (New York: Harcourt Brace Jovanovich 1978), p. 314.

10. Jean-Francois Lyotard, *The Differend* (Minneapolis: University of Minnesota Press, 1988), p. 76.

11. John W. Murphy, *Postmodern Social Analysis and Criticism* (Westport, CT: Greenwood Press, 1989), pp. 19–21.

12. Merleau-Ponty, *The Visible and the Invisible*, p. 248.

13. Lyotard, *The Postmodern Condition*, p. 10.

14. Lyotard, *The Differend*, pp. 32-58.

15. Diana Fuss, *Essentially Speaking* (New York: Routledge, 1989), pp. 2-6.

16. Lyotard, *The Postmodern Condition*, p. 59.

17. Stanley Cohen, *Visions of Social Control* (Cambridge: Polity Press, 1985), pp. 87-114.

18. Goffman, *Asylums*.

19. Jean Gebser, *The Ever-Present Origin* (Athens, OH: Ohio University Press, 1985), p. 544.

20. Lyotard, *The Postmodern Condition*, pp. 58-59.

21. Guattari, *Molecular Revolution*, p. 93.

22. William A. Vega and John W. Murphy, *Culture and the Restructuring of Community Mental Health* (Westport, CT: Greenwood Press, 1990), pp. 92-95.

23. John W. Murphy, John T. Pardeck, and Karen A. Callaghan, "The Ecological Model, Holism, and Socially Sensitive Counseling," *International Journal of Adolescence and Youth* 1(2) (1988): pp. 173-184.

24. Ludwig Von Bertalanffy, *Perspectives on General Systems Theory* (New York: George Braziller, 1975), pp. 97-102.

25. John W. Murphy and Karen A. Callaghan, "Systems Theory and the Family: A Critique," *Early Child Development and Care* (39) (1988): pp. 163-176.

26. Deleuze and Guattari, *On the Line*, pp. 10-20.

27. Gebser, *The Ever-Present Origin*, pp. 309-310.

28. Deleuze and Guattari, *On the Line*, p. 15.

29. Jean-Francois Lyotard, "The Tensor," in *The Lyotard Reader*, ed. Andrew Benjamin (London: Basil Blackwell, 1989), pp. 1-18.

30. John W. Murphy and John T. Pardeck "The 'Burnout Syndrome' and Management Style," *The Clinical Supervisor* 4(4) (1986): pp. 35-44.

31. Namm, "The Case of the Changing Technology: Impact of Microcomputer Technology in a *Fortune* 500 Company," in *Technology and Human Productivity*, pp. 95-111.

32. Kanter, *The Change Masters*, p. 137.

33. Joyce Rothschild and J. Allen Whitt, *The Cooperative Workplace* (Cambridge: Cambridge University Press, 1986).

34. Michel Foucault, *The Archaeology of Knowledge* (London: Routledge, 1989), p. 177.

35. Alfred Schutz and Thomas Luckmann, *The Structures of the Life-World* (Evanston, IL: Northwestern University Press, 1973), pp. 21-98.

36. Heim, *Electric Language: A Philosophical Study of Word Processing*, p. 99.

# 10

---

# Conclusion: Calculating versus Thinking

The Dreyfuses write that the optimism witnessed among many researchers in the field of artificial intelligence has begun to wane.[1] During the 1950s scholars such as Newell, Shaw, and Simon, for example, believed that even the activities of the mind would soon be computerized. As techniques improved, they assumed there would be nothing that computers would be unable to do. Yet a sort of mundane notion has stifled progress, something that technicians were likely to overlook. Simply put, the issue of common sense knowledge has proven to be very problematic.[2]

In fact, the difficulties posed by common sense will be the next challenge researchers will have to overcome, argues Minsky. In this regard, the Dreyfuses report that Winograd spends a lot of his time teaching Heidegger to students, in order to resurrect the epistemological side of computerization. The issue of common sense has also become a major theme in social sciences such as sociology, due to interest that has been expressed recently in G. H. Mead, Blumer, Garfinkle, and a host of newer European theorists.[3] What these writers argue is that the social world is seriously misrepresented by the model of objective rationality that has been traditionally cited to support computerization.[4] They claim social interaction cannot be summarized in this rationalistic manner without an appreciable loss of meaning.

By emphasizing common sense the aim is to illustrate that knowledge is socially constructed. Winograd and Flores make this point when they contend that a person makes decisions in terms of his or her "task environment and internal representation."[5] As a result, logic is never pure but is always incomplete, selective, and provisional. Rather than based on so-called empirical regularities, rationality has a pragmatic thrust. Reason, in other words, is context-bound. Accordingly, Weizenbaum remarks that understanding requires a "global context." He writes that a "conversation proceeds by establishing sub-contexts, a sub-context within these, and so on."[6]

Clearly, the practice of intervention would benefit from the insight associated with understanding common sense. Practitioners should be reminded constantly that human experience is not a closed system, fixed or oriented in terms of unambiguous rules or referents. Deviance or illness, therefore, is not necessarily a state that can be easily delineated. These are not abstractions, but, as Wittgenstein says, "forms of life."[7] Obviously this is the case to anyone who has worked in a social service agency. How clients define their situation greatly influences their acceptance of a diagnosis and their view of treatment, in addition to the probable outcome of intervention. Ignoring the dimension of common sense would therefore appear to be a serious mistake.

But instead of becoming community-based, practitioners are being encouraged to move in the exact opposite direction. As a consequence of increased computerization, the gradual adoption of an "elitist" model is occurring.[8] A way of thinking is becoming accepted that fosters reliance on experts and technicians, while transforming knowledge into abstract data. Weizenbaum warns that "we have permitted technological metaphors . . . and technology itself to so thoroughly pervade our thought processes that we have finally abdicated to technology the very duty to formulate questions."[9] Yet practitioners always encounter their clients *in situ*, and thus intervention should always be viewed as a human enterprise. Technical acuity, in short, is no substitute for intimacy and cultural sensitivity. Nonetheless, the tendency has been to treat computers as autonomous machines, rather than look for human-centered approaches to computerization.[10]

Computerization and common sense represent completely different principles. One is constrictive and the others is expansive; one is mechanical and the other is interpretive; one is formal and the other is concrete. In fact, the purpose of computerization is to extract knowledge from its context in order to make the flow of information more efficient. However, the result is an ersatz portrayal of social life. Undoubtedly, practitioners should not be interested in a model or any methodology that deanimates service delivery. Why would socially inappropriate services ever be desirable? Stated differently, why is a model encouraged that may undermine the development of a socially appropriate intervention? The desire to be accepted as a science provides a partial answer.

Nonetheless, those who deliver services must never be lulled into thinking that precision, efficiency, and comprehensiveness are in themselves the traits of a good intervention. For these notions may not be helpful at all unless they are underpinned by an attempt to be relevant. If an intervention is not attuned correctly to how persons interpret their behavior, even a comprehensive treatment regimen may be perceived as intrusive and unresponsive to their needs. But practitioners must not forget that relevancy is not usually thought to be a primary characteristic of computerization.

In many respects, computerization is antithetical to relevancy. If the term *relevance* means a concern for particulars, nuances, and local definitions, computerization is obviously inconsistent with that idea. Clearly, eliminating these contingencies from data processing is the purpose of computerization. What this essentially means is that computers are primordially reductionistic. In this regard, F. H. George concludes that these devices are "selective processors."[11]

But practitioners can easily get swept up by the technological zeitgeist. As a result, they do not really strive to make computer technology socially responsible. Instead, the argument is often made that improved training, increased technical acuity, and the unbiased administration of tests and other clinical instruments are sufficient for this task. The caveat is often heard from technicians that the manufacturers of computers are not responsible for the incompetence of those who use these devices. Primarily, interference from non-technical elements, in other words, is thought to reduce the effectiveness of computer technology.

Throughout this book the exact opposite claim is made: non-technical involvement is integral to the proper, or humane, use of computers. As Michie and Johnston advise, computer technology should be adjusted to what they call the "human window."[12] This is the "narrow band where both the processing capability and the scales of memory are equivalent to those possessed by humans." When this is accomplished the alienating effects of computerization will be reduced; human experience will not be confronted by an ominous adversary.

Nonetheless, there are obvious limits to how completely experience and computerization can be merged. Typically, computers are thought to be most applicable to structured tasks; nonstructured tasks are assumed difficult to computerize.[13] Yet, even in very structured situations, the categories adopted to classify events are, almost by definition, not isomorphic with reality. Considering that choices, definitions, and commitments are central to every aspect of existence, how can a complete picture of reality, or a comprehensive computer program, ever be produced? For example, beliefs cannot be easily circumscribed because they are constantly changing, due to their interpretive character. In this sense, allegedly structured situations are not necessarily more reliably programmed than any other, for every task is underpinned by social assumptions that cannot be unconditionally generalized. Complete isomorphism between a computer program and social reality will thus always elude programmers and system design experts. This is true even when an assignment, such as garnering demographic information, appears to be quite simple.

What practitioners should never forget is that intervention is replete with epistemological considerations. Questions such as, What is the context of knowledge? How does interpretation affect the nature of data? How are deviance and normalcy socially constructed? What is the social logic used to classify events? are never irrelevant. For example, a person's sexual or ethnic identity, which was once thought to be relatively easy to ascertain, is now often difficult to classify neatly.

Obviously, technical and epistemological questions are not the same and should never be confused. Although epistemology may be disturbing to technicians, for abstract system building is discouraged, this critical reflection should not be viewed as incompatible with intervention. Indeed, how can relevant services be offered without any interest in the status of knowledge? Because social and computer space are not identical, intervention should not be misunderstood to take place within a pristine environment. The identity of knowledge, in short, should always be approached as questionable by practitioners.

Therefore, advise Winograd and Flores, practitioners should work within the "space of potential breakdowns."[14] This does not mean they should simply increase their tolerance for faults, because computer technology is complex, fragile, and susceptible to malfunctions. Instead, and much more significant, Winograd and Flores argue that practitioners should recognize that moving from one domain of common sense to another can cause a breakdown in computerization. The Dreyfuses call this "changing relevance."[15] This is the same point made by Thom with his catastrophe theory, when he demonstrates that dramatic shifts in logic are not uncommon and culminate in altering what is accepted to be real.

Winograd and Flores, in their own inimitable way, are also calling for practitioners to become reflexive. But practitioners should recognize that formalization will not achieve this end. In fact, potential epistemological breaks are concealed by formalization, in order to create the illusion of a smoothly operating system.

What is needed for successful intervention is not an image of reality, but access to the common sense that guides a community's actions. Yet basic to computerization is an agreement about what constitutes reason, facts, and an appropriate range of questions about knowledge. In the social world, however, this type of consensus rarely exists pertaining to issues such as illness, deviance, and successful rehabilitation. And since the passage of the Community Mental Health Act, uniform definitions of illness behavior, for example, are not expected to be discovered. Therefore, socially sensitive measures are supposed to be used in identifying and formulating solutions to problems. The allure of technology should not blind practitioners to this need.

The point is that practitioners should always be epistemologists. This alliance may cause technical problems, but the resulting difficulties are well worth the price. After all, in the balance are the lives of clients! And when practitioners fail to remember the human side of intervention, they become nothing more than technocrats.

Technocrats calculate, practitioners think. In other words, technocrats classify, differentiate, and allocate resources. Practitioners, on the other hand, are supposed to understand, recognize uniqueness, and offer aid. The general outlook supported by technology should not be allowed to blur these distinctions. What could be worse than practitioners becoming technocrats? Hence, practitioners should recognize there are no hard and fast rules for engaging communities.

To the technocrat, socially sensitive intervention must appear to be inefficient, for well circumscribed search strategies are not usually followed. Often seemingly conflicting practices are tried. Nonetheless, formalizing the intervention process may be efficient but ineffective, which is clearly an unacceptable trade-off. Additional analytical training, furthermore, is not a corrective, if the current computer schemes are socially inadequate.

Formalization is not an appropriate philosophy to guide intervention, claim the Dreyfuses, for a simple reason.[16] Portraying humans as rational animals no longer makes sense. In this regard, the Dreyfuses join the ranks of postmodernists, who acknowledge that humans are far more than rational. Humans, in short, are always developing and thus have no beginning or end point. And because their growth has no inherent direction, the behavior of persons is multivalent, surprising, and maybe most important, subject to interpretation. Given this description, allowing formalization to direct the conceptualization, delivery, and evaluation of services can only be assessed as foolhardy. Therefore, this reductionistic philosophy—in the guise of computerization—should be seriously reevaluated in terms of its ability to sustain intervention, and, accordingly, service delivery should not be allowed to assume a technical cast.

## NOTES

1. Dreyfus and Dreyfus, *Mind Over Machine*, pp. 67-100.
2. Donald Michie and Rory Johnston, *The Knowledge Machine* (New York: William Morrow and Company, 1985), p. 17.
3. John W. Murphy, "Recent Trends in Sociological Theory," *Research Journal of Philosophy and Social Science* (in press).

4. Herbert A. Simon, *Administrative Behavior* (New York: The Free Press, 1976), p. 67.

5. Winograd and Flores, *Understanding Computers and Cognition*, p. 23.

6. Joseph Weizenbaum, "Contextual Understanding by Computers," in *Recognizing Patterns: Studies in Living and Automatic Systems*, ed. Paul A. Kolers and Murray Eden (Cambridge: MIT Press, 1988), p. 181.

7. Ludwig Wittgenstein, *Philosophical Investigations* (Oxford: Basil Blackwell, 1953), p. 226.

8. Vega and Murphy, *Culture and the Restructuring of Community Mental Health*, pp. 130-133.

9. Joseph Weizenbaum, "On the Impact of the Computer on Society," *Science* 176(12) (1972): p. 611.

10. Karamjit S. Gill, "The Knowledge-Based Machine: Issues of Knowledge Transfer," in *Artificial Intelligence for Society*, ed. Karamjit S. Gill (Chichester: John Wiley and Sons, 1986), p. 13.

11. F. H. George, *Philosophical Foundations of Cybernetics* (Kent, Great Britain: Abacus, 1979), p. 79.

12. Michie and Johnston, *The Knowledge Machine*, p. 78.

13. Winograd and Flores, *Understanding Computers and Cognition*, p. 153.

14. Ibid., p. 73.

15. Dreyfus and Dreyfus, *Mind Over Machine*, p. 79.

16. Ibid., pp. 202-206.

# Selected, Annotated Bibliography

Barrett, William, *The Illusion of Technique*. Garden City, NY: Anchor Press, 1978. The conceptual and practical limitations of technology are the focus of attention.

————. *Death of the Soul: From Descartes to the Computer*. New York: Doubleday, 1986. Traditional Western philosophy is shown to culminate in the reification of human action and thought.

Boden, Margaret, *Artificial Intelligence and Natural Man*. New York: Basic Books, 1977. A noted psychologist provides insight into the human significance of artificial intelligence.

Bolter, J. David, *Turing's Man: Western Culture in the Computer Age*. Chapel Hill: University of North Carolina Press, 1984. Bolter illustrates how computer technology shapes the ways in which persons think about practically every aspect of culture.

Borgmann, Albert, *Technology and the Character of Contemporary Life*. Chicago: University of Chicago Press, 1984. A discussion of the philosophical presuppositions of technology is provided.

Burnham, David, *The Rise of the Computer State*. New York: Random House, 1983. Addresses the notion that the widespread use of computers may stifle the flow of information and concentrate power in a small group of technical experts.

Cnaan, Ram, and Phyllida Parsloe, eds., *The Impact of Information Technology on Social Work Practice*. New York: Haworth, 1989. Addresses the problems of linking the various new technologies to social work practice.

Dery, David, *Computers in Welfare*. Beverly Hills: Sage, 1981. Makes the case that computers may only increase bureaucracy in an agency unless the proper policies are adopted to prevent this travesty.

Dreyfus, Hubert L., *What Computers Can't Do*. New York: Harper and Row, 1972. Examines the incongruency between the mind and computers.

Dreyfus, Hubert L., and Stuart E. Dreyfus, *Mind over Machine*. New York: Free Press, 1986. The inability of expert systems to mimic the decision making ability of human experts is analyzed.

Ellul, Jacques, *The Technological Society*. New York: 1964. A classic statement on the problems facing a society dominated by technology.

Feigenbaum, Edward, and Pamela McCorduck, *The Fifth Generation: Artificial Intelligence and Japan's Computer Challenge to the World*. Lexington, MA: Addison-Wesley, 1983. Offers an assessment of Japan's technical advancements and the policies adopted by Japanese officials to promote growth in the area of computer technology.

Hatt, Harold, *Cybernetics and the Image of Man*. Nashville: Abington Press, 1968. Discussed is how the advent of cybernetics altered the ways persons view themselves, ethical issues, nature, and the social environment.

Haugeland, John, ed., *Mind Design*. Montgomery, VT: Bradford Books, 1981. Discusses of the problems encountered by those who try to design intelligent machines by various experts.

————, *Artificial Intelligence: The Very Idea*. Cambridge: Bradford/MIT Press, 1985. The concept of artificial intelligence is subjected to intense scrutiny.

Heim, Michael, *Electric Language: A Philosophical Study of Word Processing*. New Haven: Yale University Press, 1987. Addresses the question, How does word processing dehumanize and thus distort writing?

Hookway, Christopher, ed., *Minds, Machines, and Evolution*. Cambridge: Cambridge University Press, 1984. Addresses the feasibility of comparing machines to humans.

Leiss, William, *The Domination of Nature*. Boston: Beacon Press, 1974. Illustrates how technology is able to eviscerate nature.

McCorduck, Pamela, *Machines Who Think*. San Francisco: W. H. Freeman, 1979. Provides a comprehensive history of artificial intelligence.

Mumford, Lewis, *Technics and Civilization*. New York: Harcourt, Brace, and World, 1963. An early assessment of how technology can systematically destroy communities, nature, and other key aspects of culture.

Murphy, John W., Algis Mickunas, and Joseph J. Pilotta, eds., *The Underside of High-Tech*. Westport, CT: Greenwood, 1986. The impact of the computer world-view on a wide range of social institutions.

Murphy, John W., and John T. Pardeck, eds., *Technology and Human Productivity: Challenges for the Future*. Westport, CT: Greenwood, 1986. The findings of a conference devoted to exploring the relationship between increased technological development and productivity.

——, *Technology and Human Services Delivery*. New York: Haworth, 1988. Provides a critical look at the ways in which the human element may be removed from service delivery as a by-product of computerizing agencies.

Papert, Seymour, *Mindstorms: Children, Computers, and Powerful Ideas*. New York: Basic Books, 1980. Analyzes of the role computers can play in helping children to master difficult ideas and procedures.

Pardeck, John T., and John W. Murphy, eds., *Computers in Human Services: An Overview for Clinical and Welfare Services*. London: Harwood Academic Publishers, 1990. Addresses the conceptual side of implementing and using computer technology.

——, *Microcomputers in Early Childhood Education*. New York: Gordon and Breach Science Publishers, 1989. Focuses on the influence of microcomputer technology in early childhood education.

Pardeck, John T., and John W. Murphy, "Technology and the Therapeutic Relationship," *Family Therapy* 13 (1) (1986). Special issue devoted to investigating the impact of technology on family intervention.

Pratt, Vernon, *Thinking Machines*. Oxford: Basil Blackwell, 1987. Outlines the history of computers, along with an examination of the theoretical changes that took place at each stage of their development.

Ringle, Martin, ed., *Philosophical Perspectives in Artificial Intelligence*. Atlantic Highlands, NJ: Humanities Press, 1979. Addresses various philosophical questions in terms of creating computers that can mimic human cognition.

Roszak, Theodore, *The Cult of Information*. New York: Pantheon Books, 1986. Discusses how knowledge, intelligence, and related issues have been redefined in the so-called Computer Age.

Schank, Roger C., and R.P. Abelson, *Scripts, Plans, Goals, and Understanding*. Hillsdale, NJ: Lawrence Erlbaum Associates, 1977. Discusses a novel approach to computerizing the knowledge persons use in everyday life to organize daily affairs.

Schoech, Dick, *Computer Use in Human Services: A Guide to Information Management*. New York: Human Sciences Press, 1982. A compendium of ways computers can be used to streamline and improve service delivery.

Schwartz, Marc D., ed., *Using Computers in Clinical Practice*. New York: Haworth Press, 1984. Examines of a plethora of computer applications to clinical practice.

Shallis, Michael, *The Silicon Idol*. Oxford: Oxford University Press, 1984. Critiques the role played by computers in the operation of the modern world.

Sidowski, Joseph B., James H. Johnson, and Thomas A. Williams, eds., *Technology in Mental Health Care Delivery Systems*. Norwood, NJ: Ablex, 1980. Offers a positive view of how computer technology can facilitate intervention by health care providers.

Simon, Herbert, *The Sciences of the Artificial*. 2nd ed. Cambridge: MIT Press, 1981. Attempts to justify, in both theoretical and practical terms, the study of artificial intelligence.

Sloman, Aaron, *The Computer Revolution in Philosophy*. Atlantic Highlands, NJ: Humanities Press, 1978. Addresses the philosophical problems posed by computerization.

Turkle, Sherry, *The Second Self: Computers and the Human Spirit*. New York: Simon and Schuster, 1984. Questions the intellectual framework and cultural outlook adopted by those who use computers.

Weiner, Norbert, *Cybernetics*. Cambridge: MIT Press, 1961. Outlines the philosophical principles that underpin this version of systems theory.

Weizenbaum, Joseph, *Computer Power and Human Reason*. San Francisco: W. H. Freeman, 1976. One of the first critiques on the dehumanizing effects of computerization.

Winograd, Terry, *Understanding Natural Language*. New York: Academic Press, 1972. Represents Winograd's early attempt to deal with the problems associated with computerizing natural language.

Winograd, Terry, and Fernando Flores, *Understanding Computers and Cognition*. Norwood, NJ: Ablex, 1986. Computerization is discussed in terms of the advances made in modern philosophy.

Winner, Langdon, *Autonomous Technology*. Cambridge: MIT Press, 1977. Describes the political implications of technology.

# Index

## About the Authors

JOHN W. MURPHY is Associate Professor of Sociology at the University of Miami. Among the many books he has written are *Postmodernism Social Analysis and Criticism* (Greenwood Press, 1989) and, with John T. Pardeck, *Technology and Human Productivity* (Greenwood Press, 1986).

JOHN T. PARDECK is Professor of Social Work at Southeast Missouri State University. He has authored or coauthored numerous books, including *Technology and Human Productivity* (Greenwood Press, 1986), *Books for Early Childhood: A Developmental Perspective* (Greenwood Press, 1986), and *Young People with Problems: A Guide to Bibliotherapy* (Greenwood Press, 1984).